The Art AND SCIENCE OF _Success_

VOLUME 3

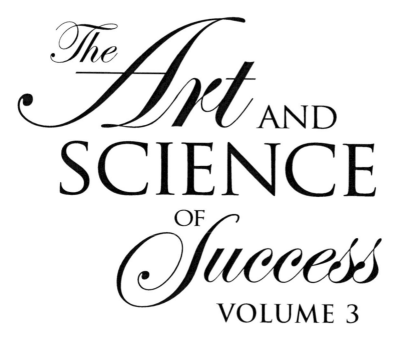

The Art AND SCIENCE OF Success

VOLUME 3

PROVEN STRATEGIES FROM
TODAY'S LEADING EXPERTS

SUCCESS YOU PUBLISHING
CARROLLTON, TX

SUCCESS YOU PUBLISHING

Success You Publishing, Inc.
2810 Trinity Mills Road #209-142
Carrollton, TX 75006
questions@mattmorris.com

ISBN: 978-0-9830770-2-2

Printed in United States of America

Cover Design: Chris Collins
Interior Design & Layout: Ghislain Viau

Contents

Foreword

Congratulations on picking up this book! The simple fact that you're reading this puts you among the top 5% in the world who are likely to achieve what they really want out of life.

I firmly believe that most people die at the age of about 35. . . . They're just not buried for several more decades—except in their own ruts. The majority of our worldwide population is stuck in the rut of life. For some it may be a deep rut, and for others it may be shallow, but nonetheless, we all have a part of our life that is not where we want it to ultimately be.

You may know what I'm talking about. . . . Going to work every day to a job that doesn't fulfill you, being involved in a relationship that doesn't excite you, walking around in a body that you're not proud of, struggling with anxiety, depression, lack of self-confidence, money, and the list goes on and on.

I have good news and bad news.

The bad news is that there is no magic formula. As great as this book is, and as powerful as our coauthors are, you're probably not going to read it and then suddenly "arrive" at where you want to be in life.

Heck of a sales pitch coming from the publisher of the book, eh?

The reality is, no book in the world is going to turn you into an overnight success and give you unlimited happiness, total confidence, endless fulfillment, the motivation to create your ideal body, perfect relationships, and financial riches.

The good news is this. . . .

Through the insights, principles, and proven strategies outlined in this book, along with our other volumes of *The Art & Science of Success*, your life will be taken to another level. It may not happen overnight, but through the process of consistent learning, you *will* see remarkable changes in your life when you commit to reading and applying what you learn in this book.

The Art & Science of Reading This Book

Here's my simple advice on how to read this book:

Commit to one chapter a day.

That's it.

Each chapter is approximately 1,500–2,000 words and should not take you any longer than about 10 to 15 minutes to read. A chapter a day is easy to do. But it's also easier *not* to do. Which is why you must **commit**.

Here's my definition of commitment:

Doing the thing you said you would do long after the feeling you said it in is over.

If you're willing to give up any excuses and commit to just one chapter a day, you will begin to see a significant shift in your life over time. In other words, approach this book with a scientific consistency and you will be able to create a masterpiece of success in your own life.

What radically changed my life and allowed me to go from homeless, $30,000 in debt, and miserable to becoming a self-made millionaire and living what has been a dream life over the last decade has largely come from my commitment to this 10-minute-a-day philosophy.

Over the last 13 years, I've read literally hundreds of books. You see, I never experienced instant success. But what happened over the years, through this consistent commitment, is that I've simply gotten a little bit better every week over a long period.

Einstein said the greatest invention in the history of the world is compound interest. The same principle applies to your success—it's called compound intelligence.

Becoming 1% better every week over time will dramatically change your life forever because you will have an intelligence, a success IQ, that is far superior to that of everyone else in the world.

The Art & Science of Success is a breakthrough in the personal development publishing industry. Rather than publishing an entire 50,000–60,000-word book by one author, we are taking the absolute best of the best content from today's leading experts on success.

Each of our experts has made an art form of achieving success in particular areas and in life, and each has written one powerful chapter allowing you to discover their no-B.S., no-fluff strategies for experiencing transformational success in every way imaginable.

The Art & Science of Success gives you the most cutting-edge and modern techniques for increasing your financial wealth, your spiritual abundance, your personal fulfillment and happiness, your health and vitality, your relationships, your marketing and business skills, and much, much more.

Each of our authors has a commitment to your success. Should you find particular authors who impact you, feel free to reach out to them via their websites or contact details listed at the end of their chapter.

Congratulations again on picking up this book. Now's the time to get to work and start reading! If you consistently commit to reading just a chapter a day, your life will never be the same again.

—Matt Morris

Chapter 1

Never Give Up on Your Business Success

By Steve Little

*H*ave you ever felt like you're ready to quit? Just ready to give up on the whole idea of finding and building a business? Pass on the idea of securing true wealth and financial security for yourself and your children?

Are you frustrated beyond words . . . fed up . . . disappointed . . . disillusioned . . . disheartened?

Are you wondering why in the heck it seems that everything is so dang difficult?

It's okay. I've had this feeling plenty of times. In fact, all successful people do. It sort of goes with the territory. *Believe it or not, it's actually a REALLY good sign.*

One important key to your business success is how you deal with these thoughts and emotions. It is one of what I call the "refiner fires of success." It weeds out the truly success-bound from the wannabes.

I'm going to show you how to respond like a wildly successful entrepreneur and share one profound truth and give you one very simple instruction. If you'll trust me and do what I tell you to do, you'll never be tempted to choose failure over success again.

This one little tip has saved my bacon hundreds, no thousands, of times . . . in business . . . in athletics . . . in racing . . . in relationships . . . in everything.

A countless number of times the recollection of this simple truth has ultimately made the difference between success and failure for me. And I have it on excellent authority that the same goes for many, many other successes as well.

It is a phrase that is often attributed the wisdom of a Chinese proverb. I can't prove that it is, but I can assure you that if you can keep it in mind when you are frustrated or struggling, then it is guaranteed to pull you through to the success you desire.

The phrase is simply this:

"The temptation to quit will be greatest just before you're about to succeed."

Or, as my friend Bob Parsons, founder of Go Daddy, paraphrases:

"When you're ready to quit, you're closer than you think."

Or maybe you've heard it this way:

"It's always darkest just before the dawn."

Regardless which resonates with you, if you'll keep this one simple truth in mind, you'll never be truly tempted to quit. Here are some ways to keep it ever-present in your mind for those times you need it. Any and all of them work, so give them a try:

- Configure the expression of your choice as the text of your computer screen saver.
- Write it on a Post-it Note and stick it on your computer screen or keyboard.
- Post it on a note in today's calendar entry.
- Write it on a 3" x 5" card and tape it to the wall right above your office light switch.
- Write it along the top of the whiteboard in your office.
- Tape it to the sun visor in your car.

Is it "magic"? No, not really. . . . It is just a simple truth we all tend to forget when we are in the midst of a trial. These are simple ways to remind you when you need it most.

Look, anyone who tells you that there will not be trials along the way in life and business is not telling you the truth. I think you know that.

The difference between successful people and the rest is that successful people find ways to move past the struggle, break through the trial, and remain focused on the prize. Even simple little tips and tricks like this one have a profound effect.

Don't discount it just because it does not seem a grand enough measure to assure success. In the end, people do not fail without choosing . . . whether consciously or not.

Using anything that works for you will keep you from choosing failure over business success. Let me know which one you use and how it works for you.

I'm standing for all that's possible for you in life and business.

Biography

Steve Little

As a dedicated husband and father, champion athlete, author, skilled craftsman, accomplished musician, and acclaimed veteran entrepreneur, STEVE LITTLE understands the critical importance of finding and designing your business or vocation so that it serves and delivers the achievement of all the things you are purposefully committed to accomplishing in *all* areas of life.

He regularly advises business owners on how to develop key inner resources, the mental capacity for success, and the vital personal success skills necessary to generate powerful advantage-making strategies and to win big in both life and business.

Steve helps wannabe business owners, early stage entrepreneurs, as well as established business owners and corporate leadership overcome the myriad complex challenges they face and develop breakthrough strategies for finding, designing, organizing, and building a business that grows rapidly to provide the satisfying and rewarding financial and lifestyle returns they expect and deserve.

His mission, purpose, and unwavering commitment are to help you enjoy owning the wildly successful business of your dreams.

Steve has been building successful businesses for nearly four decades. In that time, he's enjoyed a multitude of successful ventures of virtually all kinds. Everything from his first commercial venture at age 13, which sold a few years later for a handsome six-figure sum, to successful venture capital-backed software companies, which he helped grow to generate hundreds of millions of dollars in revenue, produce dramatic returns for investors, and employ thousands of people worldwide. He's built just as many wildly successful home-based, lifestyle businesses too.

Throughout the past 10 years, Steve has personally coached hundreds of business owners, executives, and corporate leadership teams to astonishing levels of personal and professional success. He is a highly sought-after business success leader, adviser, mentor, and coach. He is recognized as one of the leading experts in developing peak individual and team performance.

He's learned a thing or two about success and how to achieve it. And now he's made it his personal mission to share what he knows about success in business (and in life) with you.

Contact Information

www.howtobeginabusiness.com
www.theperfectbizfinder.com
www.theperfectbizbuildercoaching.com

Chapter 2
Pay It Forward

By Bill Walsh

I'm sure that you've heard of the concept "pay it forward." Maybe you've even seen the movie *Pay It Forward*. Well, many years ago, I was in a movie based on a similar philosophy called *Pass It On*. It was all about paying it forward, making a difference, and helping people.

Most people don't believe in that concept. You may believe that if you help enough people get what they want, you'll also get what you want. Zig Ziglar talked about that many, many years ago. Most people still don't believe it.

They're programmed to believe that you work and get a check as soon as you've done the work. That really is the wrong mindset if you want to build an exceptional company or live a life of brilliance. The problem with that mentality, or programming, is that it only works for someone *without* a bigger vision, *without* a bigger passion, and *without* a bigger inspiration to make a difference on the planet.

When you pay it forward, the universe yields what's possible—but only if *you* believe it's possible. If you're thinking about how to truly grow your business and live way on the other side of what is possible, it starts with *you* believing that when you pay it forward, it works.

I know this is hard to understand until you see it firsthand. I've seen people create more success by helping others first. Not only did they help them, they offered the help *in advance*.

Here's the key, the answer to the $64,000 question: it takes WORK to achieve success. Working to help others is work that eventually comes back to you. Help others *first* by providing value that matters to the person you're helping (without expecting anything in return), and it will come back to you a hundredfold. Have faith—it works!

As you start to live in a place of helping other people first who play at a much higher level, watch how things start to come back to you. If you want to create more income, help other people create success.

The Bible offers two words to describe what to do: Serve others. When you serve others on a massive scale, it comes back to you massively—including achieving absolute wealth.

John F. Kennedy talked about the same thing regarding serving others, right? He said, "Ask not what your country can do for you. Ask what you can do for your country." Do not expect anything in return. Go out of your way to help others first and watch the magnificent universe yield for you. The only thing I would add to this concept is that paying it forward feels phenomenal.

How many times did you pay it forward this week? Go out of your way for the next 14 days to help other people with no expectation of money or reward. In just 14 days, you can create habits. It's amazing what happens when you start to help other people first. They will realize you're coming from a genuine place, a place of service.

Remember how Mother Teresa would never, ever go to an antiwar rally, but if there was a peace rally, she'd be the first one in attendance? You've got to be the first one in attendance to doing things differently and positively today.

Right now, as you read this, what are you doing to figure out specifically how you can help people over the next 14 days? If you want to connect with high-level people, if you want to do more business, you need to go out to the marketplace with people who are doing better than you, and ask yourself: "How can I truly help that person? How can I bring value to their life first and expect nothing in return?" Do more deals. Do more joint ventures. Have more fun. Wow, what a concept!

Think about a time in your life when you went out of your way to help somebody. You made a difference for that person. Even though you were not doing it to receive anything in return, good came back to you. It's the same whether you are making a difference for someone on a personal level or in business.

If you truly want to grow your business, and you want to have more fun in your life, figure out at least three to five people that you can go out of your way to help in some way. Do it today!

This task can be a tough one. When we meet really successful people, so often we're star struck. We're not sure what to say. In high school or college, did you take that class called, "How to Connect with Millionaires"? No, of course not—because they didn't offer it.

When opportunity shows up for most people, you know what they do? They freeze. If I dropped you into a room full of millionaires and billionaires and said go connect with them, you would probably be afraid of what to say and how to interact.

I'll teach you to understand this process of connecting with high-level people with absolute faith. That's right, with absolute faith. There's no room for fear.

One of the core secrets is not doing what most people do when they meet successful people. What they do (that you don't want to do) is start babbling about themselves. Here's my car; here's what I do; here's my business; and on and on. That doesn't work. What *does* work is asking them about themselves and *listening for ways to create value first and expect nothing in return.* Then follow up on providing that value.

Here's a great example. More than five years ago, I had a chance to meet a gentleman named Mark Victor Hansen. As one of the co-authors of the *Chicken Soup for the Soul* series, he's written lots of successful books.

When I met him, I said hello and shook his hand at a charity fundraiser. I had donated to the charity because I knew he was someone who lives in a place of brilliance. His focus is to inspire the planet and make the world a better place—every day. I loved what he was about and his message.

After we met, nothing really happened. I didn't have the right connections or the right way to open the door. A year went by. Then two years. Finally, Mark and I connected through another gentleman, Robert Allen. They were writing a new book and would most likely be coming to Chicago as part of their book tour. I let them know that I believed in them and their message.

I told them that if they were coming to Chicago, I'd love to help promote their book. I added that I could probably put a group together that would buy whatever books they brought. I asked for nothing in return. They didn't call back right away. They weren't sure if they would be in Chicago. A month went by and soon it was two weeks before the event.

One of the things required to become successful is to be persistent. So, I called again to follow up. It was just a few days before they were going to be in Chicago. They did need my help in putting together a lunch. I let them know that we would buy whatever books they brought.

So, I got focused and made calls to more than one hundred people I knew I could count on to be at the lunch, even though it was last-minute notice. I let everyone I invited know the details of the event and that they *absolutely* had to be there.

Because I had previously done a great job of creating value for my friends and my associates, I was able to pull together the event quickly so that Mark Victor Hansen and Robert Allen could spend time with world-class people who are making a difference on the planet.

When Mark and Bob showed up, they were totally blown away by how full the whole room was on short notice. This event was the first time Mark Victor Hansen and I were formally introduced. He was blown away by the quality of the people who were there. Literally every book that they brought— and they brought cases of all their books—was sold.

They asked how I could have pulled together such an event in just three days. I explained that I had created massive value first. By making it a best practice to create massive value, it becomes a habit, and it builds on itself.

Once again, when you create a lot of value, people understand that. I never asked them for anything, but what it developed into was a relationship. Mark now participates in many of our events. We've done several great projects together as a result of one of the core secrets of success: paying it forward.

I know it may not be easy to stomach that process because we're programmed otherwise. But as you start to live it, you'll realize how simple it is. Then, you'll realize how big the universe is and how it truly yields what's possible because you believe it's possible. Create the value in the marketplace, and suddenly the universe starts to yield.

Here's another example. We, the Chicago Bears, were going to the Superbowl. A group of us went to The Ritz Carlton in Florida right before the Bears were going to play. We were sitting down talking and drinking a new green energy drink we were working with that helps relieve stress. We were feeling stress about how the Bears would play.

One of the green drinks was sitting on the table. This gentleman walked up and just kind of butted into the conversation. He said, "Hey, what's that?" I let him know that it was a new product that helps with stress. He said he had stress and wanted to try some of it.

I said, "Sure. Here's some to enjoy. It's a fun experience." And I handed him the energy drink. We're having a good time, right?

He said, "Wow! This is pretty good." He didn't leave. He just stayed there. Then, suddenly, he walked away and came back. He said, "Hey, can my friends over there try some of it?"

I said, "Absolutely! Let me pour you a few glasses of it." He took the glasses over to them. They tried it.

Pay it forward works. Here's what happened. It was around lunchtime. He said, "Hey, why don't we go up to my place? We'll grab a drink."

I looked at the group of about eight of us and said, "OK, why not?"

We got into the elevator, and he pushed the "P" button. Now, I'm thinking it's one of two things, right? It's either the penthouse or the parking garage.

Well, the good news is that the elevator started going up—to the big penthouse, the owner's unit above the hotel. We walked into his unbelievably beautiful home, which overlooked the entire city skyline of Miami. We were blown away.

You never know what can happen from those instant connections. As we were walking around his place, we started talking about the Superbowl. He said, "As a matter of fact, I have two tickets for the game tonight." He explained that he was not going to go.

I asked, "Is there any way that I can buy those tickets from you?" Because they were unbelievable seats.

He said, "No, you can't buy them from me. They're my gift to you." You see, when you believe in what's possible, everything becomes totally possible.

You've got to be genuine in your belief. You've got to live from that place of service, not once in a while but all the time. The principle of paying it forward works in every area of your life: your relationships, your business, and making a difference on the planet.

So, if you're having a challenging time in your business right now—maybe things aren't going exactly how you want them to go; maybe you're not having enough sales; or maybe you're not getting all the right connections—take a moment and say to yourself, "Maybe I'm just not doing it right." Then find ways to pay it forward.

I can only share with you that this process has worked over and over and over in many significant deals and programs and projects because I ask better questions about how to provide value first. You'll find that successful people ask better questions. They ask specific questions.

The big question to ask yourself today is, "What specifically can I do today to create more value and help more people and expect nothing in return?"

When you pay it forward, the universe yields back. The bottom line is that when you pay it forward, it works. You'll have more fun. You'll have more success. You'll truly come from that place of service. And when you come from an authentic place of service and help others, people can tell. Be inspired. Pray. Be authentic. Go out there and pay it forward—and live your dreams.

Biography
Bill Walsh

BILL WALSH is the CEO/founder of the business coaching/venture capital firm Powerteam International. Bill hosts events all over the world, presenting with Brian Tracy, Mark Victor Hansen, Les Brown, T. Harv Ecker, Stephen Pierce, Alex Mandossian, Mike Lathigee, and several other well-respected authors, speakers, and business  coaches. He delivers a message of transformation and practical applications through life stories that empower people to understand specifically what it takes to build successful companies. As an accomplished author, speaker, radio personality, and movie celebrity, Bill has the background to connect instantly with the audience by sharing the mindset, methods, and systems required to win really big in the current economy.

For everyone who owns a business or would like to capitalize on the entrepreneurial dream, his message will enlighten them with knowledge and action principles to turn that passion into success. Bill has an extensive background in foreign currency trading, real estate development, and building businesses in more than 30 countries. Over the past two decades, his firm has specialized in helping companies launch, grow, and create exponential valuation in the market. The Rainmaker Summit and WIN University programs offered through Powerteam are designed to assist entrepreneurs in creating the focus, plans, and partnerships required to build multimillion-dollar companies.

Contact Information

http://billwalsh360.com

Chapter 3

Magic Moment

By Austin Walsh

Have you ever had a moment of magic that changed your life? Something that cataclysmically changed everything you thought you were going to do and set you on the right path, in the right direction? Really think about it.

As silly as it may seem, I want to share with you one of the major inspirations and motivators of my young life. Even better is the fact that my inspiration actually grew alongside me! How cool is that? And to take it a step further, my inspiration happens to be a game changer in the industry of publishing, media, entertainment, and social engagement.

What is my inspiration, you ask? None other than the delightful world of Harry Potter. Seems silly, right? Well, you're taking this from a 19-year-old Internet marketing pro who happens to have grown up alongside the legendary legacy of an international fictional hero.

Why is this relevant to my marketing manifesto? We'll get to that shortly. First, let me share an email I sent out on the night the last Harry Potter film premiered:

> **SUBJECT: 3 AM Harry Potter Rant? Important message read (No Links all content)**
>
> You know normally I would be talking about how the marketing behind the movie was absolutely amazing, but that has NOTHING to do with this email.
>
> I really want to talk about how "magic" absolutely changed my life.

15

When I was 7 years old I picked up the first Harry Potter book, and was totally hooked.

Let me just stop there for one second . . . My generation grew up in a period of complete change—*The Internet.*

With it came huge divorce rates, more crime, more drugs, and most importantly, *more challenges.*

Harry Potter was a massive escape for me. I grew up with Harry, Ron, and Hermione . . . At times, they were literally my inspiration to keep going.

You see, many people think I grew up in this perfect world. My dad a big-time seminar speaker, and me, his perfect son with a great business.

Truth is—

- I fought with my mom pretty much daily.
- I moved out of my house basically at 17 years old.
- I was quite the troublemaker at times.
- I thought I would be no one in this world.
- I told myself I was a waste of time.
- I could never hold any stable relationships.
- I tried to be the cool kid.
- I just wanted to be normal.

I was the biggest reason I was held back in life, relationships, and business.

Harry Potter is something as a kid I could use to escape into a world where everything was beautiful; as a teenager I used it to become stronger; and as an adult it became a stepping stone into a different world.

"Do not be perfect; be willing." I was willing to take opportunities over and over again. I was willing to fail in life, business, and relationships over and over again, so that I could succeed in bigger and better ways—over and over again.

You see, things are going to come and go, but if you truly believe in the magic and make the magic happen in your life, watch what comes knocking at your door!

I will leave you my thoughts about the ending of the series and movies. . . .

The pain, the joy, the fear of becoming an adult, of leaving the things that were precious to us behind, and turning toward who we are becoming. Harry Potter isn't about facing down evil. It's about facing ourselves.

Go Face Yourself. . . .

Austin Walsh

P.S. Reply to the email and send me your thoughts :)

Childhood is exciting, but it can also be scary. Kids today are taught so little about financial literacy, creating value in the workplace, or even the simple power they have to be creators of whole worlds of products, it's no surprise that ambition falls to the wayside of mediocrity. I was almost a victim of that mentality—I too could be going to college and getting wasted while throwing away my money on a degree that was an impulsive waste of my time.

Instead, I took the inspiration I gained from the Harry Potter series and realized the amount of power I had to change my relationships, reach my personal goals of growth, and empower myself to become financially independent. As I continued to watch the Harry Potter franchise expand, with a deepening plot and a thickening line of products, I began my own personal journey into the world of promotions, Internet marketing, and business development.

The journey was long and arduous. Just as Harry Potter needed to learn important lessons to strengthen his skills and clarify his purpose, so did I. Some of the most important lessons I learned about business and marketing were also lessons that Harry learned on his journey to defeating Voldemort:

- **Don't be afraid to fail. In fact, embrace active failure.** You fail in order to learn, to rise again, and to succeed. So what is the difference between me and another broke entrepreneur? I get back up and try again. And that's the key—practice makes perfect, and some well-devised failures can really perfect your passion while offering you the best education of your life. Harry Potter fails to defeat Voldemort for six books! Every time he comes closer to defeating him, he learns a new lesson and moves forward to ultimately defeat his greatest challenge. That's a powerful lesson for a young kid to learn!

- **Share what you do with younger kids.** Get them involved, educate them, and see how it inspires them to take action. I was blessed to have a father who shared his life's passion with me—and today I do the same thing with kids younger than I am. I don't want to see an entire generation fall victim to hopelessness and helplessness—I want to impassion them to act in freedom and joy! This was only reinforced by reading Harry Potter—Harry didn't discriminate against becoming friends with someone based on their skill level or age; in fact, he and his friends frequently taught one another how to be strong and successful.

- **If for ONE SECOND you don't like what you do, you need to stop doing it and start doing something else.** Life is too short to spend a bunch of time on something that makes you miserable, and really, no amount of money is worth the amount of time you're going to waste. You are going to work, at some capacity, for the rest of your life—you might as well do something you enjoy! On every step of Harry's journey, he needed to make the choice to pursue love or to fall into darkness. Every time he approached the brink of darkness, he had to make the conscious choice to turn away. It's easy to continue rolling with the momentum you've built—it's much harder to start over again at square one. Yet I promise you, your long-term happiness is *imperative* to your success!

- **Successful people ask very different questions.** Life can be full of riddles—the key to being a winner is gaining the ability to see things from multiple perspectives so that you can ask questions that get results. Look at every great innovation of the 21st century—where do you think those ideas came from? Naturally, they came from asking questions differently. Coincidentally, Harry's journey is covered in riddles and games—and anyone who has read the book series was surely inspired to look at problems in much the same way. Harry and his friends were constantly solving their problems by looking at them in unique ways—the conventional simply would not do in the magical wizarding world.

I'm certain there are many other people, events, movies, and books that will inspire me as I continue to grow as a person and expand my business. However, Harry Potter was my moment of magic and has silently been guiding me through the most major decisions of both my personal and my business life. The lessons I've learned will always be applicable to anything I do—whether it's launching a social media marketing campaign, developing a customer's business and brand, or simply choosing my friends and partners.

And that's what defines my magic moment: it's timeless and reciprocal. I can apply these lessons, over and over again, to any situation; I can expect that they'll guide me in the best direction, every single time. More importantly, when I share them, they just keep rippling out and changing other people's lives.

So really think back—what's your magic moment?

Biography

Austin Walsh

AUSTIN WALSH is a quickly rising tech entrepreneur and Internet marketer committed to uniquely driven sales and business education grounded in firm values. At the age of 19, he has already been featured on stages alongside some of the world's most renowned speakers and business coaches. His long-term clients include Mark Victor  Hansen, Mark Accetta, Bishop Jordan, and Gary Goldstein, among others. Austin is the cofounder and marketing face of the highly profitable membership site www.isocialacademy.com.

Contact Information

www.isocialacademy.com

Chapter 4

A Healthy Success

By Joel Therien

Like everyone else, my life has had its ups and downs, but little did I know my passion for health and fitness would have such a dramatic effect on my life.

At one point, it made me so ill I feared for my future, and yet that same low point sent me on a journey that has led me to become one of the most successful and respected marketers on the Internet. I'm now the CEO of various multimillion-dollar MLM companies, including one for health and fitness.

What a story!

It all began when I watched *The Karate Kid* with my friend as a child, and together we took up the martial art as a means of getting fit. One thing led to another and he went on to become a world class Tae-Kwon-Do champion, and I took the body building route.

At college and university, I studied exercise psychology and specialized in cardiac rehabilitation. Upon graduation, I was fortunate enough to land myself a job at the prestigious Montfort hospital in Ontario.

At this time I was also gaining a great understanding of how the body worked by training to be a successful natural body builder, meaning I didn't use any steroids to bulk up my muscles.

I competed in international competitions all over the USA and did sufficiently well to be pursued by various fitness magazines. I was also in demand as a personal trainer, so naturally I needed to look good. To maintain a low amount of body fat, I worked out regularly, drank diet soft drinks, and took various protein powders to promote muscle growth.

Unfortunately, I didn't realize that much of the stuff I was consuming contained aspartame, which is an intense artificial sweetener used to replace sugar. It's also a toxic substance, and over time I developed aspartame poisoning.

When it first struck, I just felt dizzy, but then I could hardly remember my name or how to do familiar things like find my way home when I'd been out in the car. It was a scary and depressing time, especially as it later transpired that I most likely had lead poisoning as well.

I lost a lot of weight, developed multiple chemical sensitivities, and had to give up both my work at the hospital and all my dreams of becoming a professional body builder. I was left with extreme migraines and failing liver and kidneys. It was probably the lowest point in my life, but I was determined not to become a health statistic.

Rather than rely on doctors, I turned to the Internet to try to discover what was wrong with me, and at the same time I realized that people could actually make money from their home computers. I began to study Internet and network marketing, and it opened a whole new world to me.

I realized that businesses needed an online presence if they were to survive, and while my friends and family thought me delusional, a very rich gentleman I admired greatly and who lived the lifestyle I aspired to encouraged my vision and inspired me to pursue my dreams. His name was Dr. Michael Cowpland, at that time CEO of Corel Corporation (www.corel.com).

He told me that if I didn't do it, he would, and that was the first time I realized that the only difference between a very rich and successful person and Mr. Average is the willingness to take action.

I knew I had to sell my vision to the world.

My dad gave me my first lesson in sales by sending me out as a door-to-door salesman for his local ad business. I was terrified at first and absolutely useless at bringing in new clients. However, I stuck with it and pretty soon relished the challenge. I realized that the only way to go forward is to step out of your comfort zone. It's the only way you'll ever grow. Yes, stay out of your comfort zone every day! There is plenty of security when you're six feet under the ground!

My face-to-face meetings gave me the opportunity to listen to what people actually wanted and needed. It's a lesson that's served me well throughout my business career, and my first venture was to offer local businesses web listings inside my dad's telephone directory. This was quite unique at the time because most people just had their business address listed.

The next logical step was to provide web hosting to those businesses that didn't have a web presence, and while this was incredibly popular, I soon realized that many people had no idea how to generate income from their websites even when they had them up in cyberspace.

In 2004 I introduced a downloadable web conferencing tool, which allowed website owners to communicate and interact with their clients and customers. Looking back, I can see that Hot Conference had lots of limitations, but such was the popularity of this tool, everyone wanted it.

As a result, Kiosk, my hosting company in Canada, ran out of bandwidth, and the local cable provider couldn't give us any more. We'd not only used up all our allowance but most of that assigned to the local community as well!

There was only one thing to do . . .

Move!

I had to consider my customers and think long term. As difficult as it was, I uprooted my family, most of my loyal employees and their families, and we all headed south. We weren't looking for gold like in the Wild West movies; we were looking for something far more valuable to my vision—an unlimited supply of fiber optics.

We found it in Texas, the fiber optic capital of the USA.

Here we bought some land, set up a database, and over time began to provide all the tools and services I'd personally used and knew were needed to become a successful Internet and network marketer. It was a long process, but our company continued to grow, even though we weren't actively promoting, because we kept in contact with our customers via blog posts.

Nurturing relationships is a vital component of Internet businesses, and Mike Potvin (my longtime friend and righthand man) and I regularly posted situation updates.

We've now changed our company name to GVO, which stands for Global Virtual Opportunities. We provide everything a person needs who wishes to do any form of business on the Internet, whether personal or business. Our products and services offer great value for the money, and each component has an optional global business opportunity attached.

Generally, we charge about one-tenth that of our competitors, and we are able to do this because at our database in San Antonio, Texas, we own everything, including the land, database, fiber cables, and software, so there are no third parties, middle men, or share holders to inflate prices.

However, just because our products are inexpensive doesn't mean they're low quality.

We pride ourselves on providing great software and services, which are easy to use, robust and reliable, and backed by amazing 24/7 customer support.

As CEO of GVO, I can confidently and ethically provide reseller web hosting, domain registration, auto responder services, video and audio production and storage, downtime witness, web conferencing rooms, easy blog building, professional Internet marketing training, easy prospecting systems, and global home business opportunities. I told you I listened to what people wanted and needed.

However, my main passion has always been health and fitness.

Building up my Internet business to the multimillion-dollar company it is today took a lot of hard work, and sitting behind the computer for long periods of time is not the healthiest of lifestyles.

I became acutely aware that many other people are living unhealthy lifestyles too. Lack of physical exercise and fast food diets have created an obesity and diabetes epidemic sweeping through most civilized countries.

It's a health time bomb waiting to explode.

As soon as I was able to rid myself of most of the aspartame and lead poisoning through safe chelation, healthy nutrition, and sensible exercise, and began to feel better, I decided to do something about defusing this bomb.

I teamed up with my friend Chris Reid, whom I've known since kindergarten and with whom I watched *The Karate Kid* all those years ago, and we set up the 7 Minute Workout. Launched in March 2011, this health and fitness program, which demonstrates the exact way both Chris and I have always trained, will ultimately change the health of the masses.

Requiring just seven minutes of exercise a day, three times a week, it's a program even the most hardened couch potato can manage. The balanced and targeted exercise routines build optimum muscular and skeletal health, and while the program focuses primarily on exercise, it also provides a lot of information and educational material about making healthier nutritional changes for those who want it.

The most successful part of the program, however, is the active forum, where the members offer phenomenal support and encouragement to all involved. It's incredible to see the difference simple lifestyle changes can make to people's health and lives, and I am so proud of all the members who share their successes with others.

Some of their stories are truly inspirational.

In a strange sort of way, the lowest point in my life was the catalyst for the highest point in my life, which is now.

Truly that's all any of us really has—*Now.*

You can't change the past, and you can't guarantee the future, but you can decide to make a difference in your life and the lives of others.

You just have to take action.

I did!

Biography
Joel Therien

JOEL THERIEN is the CEO of Global Virtual Opportunities and the cofounder of the revolutionary lifestyle program the 7 Minute Workout. For a more in-depth look at his rise to success, read *The GVO Story,* by his good friend Jean Shaw: www.jeanshawinterviews.com/joel7minute.html.

Contact Information

www.gogvo.com
www.gvoconference.com
www.7minuteworkout.com

Chapter 5

Dr. Doctor

by Dr. Tom Melling

On June 3, 2010, I was standing on the hills overlooking the University of Lethbridge, Canada, thinking of how far I had traveled from my childhood days in Scotland. I was waiting to have the honorary degree of doctor of laws bestowed on me, and since I was the first medical doctor to be so chosen in the history of that institution, the morning press ran the headline "Dr. Doctor."

To begin to understand my life story, we have to start in Ireland in 1845, the year of the mysterious potato blight, which, I was taught, was the cause of the famine and resultant deaths of a million souls in my country of origin. My great-grandfather and his wife were among those who fled in the face of starvation and settled around the world. My ancestors came to Scotland, and my greatest mentor, my grandfather, was born there in 1867.

I later discovered that there had been an abundance of food to sustain all those lives had it not been for the decision of the English government to export all the cattle, swine, grain, and alcohol to England, leaving the already impoverished natives to starve to death—a very well-covered-up historical holocaust. If there was protracted anger and horror at this fact, the complaints were not voiced by Grandpa William. When he was a boy, his father died of phosphorus poisoning in a Glasgow factory. At the age of 9 Grandpa William became an underground coalminer to support his mother. He told me of a rough existence, shared with women coworkers, and how glad he was to "retire" from coalmining at the age of 12 and go to work on the railroad.

Grandpa married his love, Elizabeth, and after my mother was born, Elizabeth became pregnant again soon afterwards. She was 29 when Grandpa came home to find her hemorrhaging and went by horse and buggy to fetch the doctor. When they returned, his wife and baby were lying dead on the floor. I cannot imagine that trauma, but he never married again and was devoted to raising my mother. He visited his own mother daily for the rest of her life. My mother became a private secretary and also a fine pianist.

My dad, Bill, was also a coalminer's son and a local theater acting star and singer. He worked with his father, who had become head of a large insurance company, and had four children, Bill, Alice, me, and Gerard. Life was becoming settled, and we had few problems as children. Then at age five or so, my younger brother, Gerard, developed diphtheria and a large abscess in his left lung cavity. Our family doctor, Dr. Joe, inserted a huge rubber tube into Gerard's chest and drained it with an "underwater seal" (as he explained), literally on the kitchen table. No x-rays, all by clinical examination, not like surgeons today who will not take out your appendix without a CT scan! Gerard lived, and I declared at that very second that I was going to become a doctor—yes, at age seven!

I never retracted that.

I was born in the shadows of Stirling Castle, Scotland, and attended high school there, frequently visiting the Wallace ("Braveheart") Monument on my lunch breaks. Growing up in that area, I was left in little doubt about the concepts and pursuit of freedom.

Support for my goal of becoming a doctor was scarce outside my home. My school principal scoffed at it, informing me that "my own daughter could not get accepted into medical school."

I completed high school at age 15, did some advanced courses, and on the advice of Dr. Joe (remember him?) applied to study for a science degree at Glasgow University, thereafter to transfer freely to second-year medicine.

In 1945, when Dad came back from World War II, he saw an income in coalmining and told me he would work there, and as long as I was passing all exams, he would be behind me. He also hinted that if I didn't, there was an extra pair of overalls for me!

I worked every summer on farms, brickworks, trucks, and in mental hospitals. I also had a weekend job as a wedding photographer.

Grandpa sat up reading every night till 3 a.m., and I could study only when everyone else had gone to bed. He made me coffee and sometimes put cornflakes in it, "Just to give you some extra energy." He reassured me constantly that I would make it. He was a man of great integrity, compassion, optimism, and courage. When 82 years old, he asked me to take him to Glasgow to buy a winter coat. I took him to the best clothier, and when a young man brought him a coat, he looked at it in disgust and said, "I want a coat that will last for 20 years." The salesman was stunned, so I said, "Bring him a coat that will last for 20 years!"

I graduated B.Sc. in 1952 at age 19 and was accepted into medical school. I graduated with a bachelor of medicine and surgery in 1957. I studied with the surgeon who was on the team that had operated on King George VI (*The King's Speech*) and was his intern the following year. I was then drafted as an officer into the Royal Army Medical Corps and was sent to the only active arena at the time—Cyprus. Before I left, I married my fiancée, Maureen. We reunited a year later.

In Cyprus alcohol entered my life and progressed very slowly at first.

I returned to Scotland and resumed training to become a surgeon. I was full of doubt about this path and expressed that to a classmate in med school. She said to me only once, "If anyone in this class can do it, you can." For some reason I trusted her. I became a fellow of the Royal College of Surgeons of Glasgow 1966.

Maureen and I had three boys, Michael, Allen, and Stephen, but career opportunities looked very bleak in Scotland. I saw an ad for a surgeon in Lethbridge, Canada—40 applicants and lots of delay and confusion. I was the only one to lift the phone and ask, "Do you really have a position there?" They were impressed, and I got the job on the spot. My daughter, Karen, was born in 1969 as Armstrong landed on the moon.

I became a fellow of the Royal College of Surgeons of Canada in 1972, which was an epic year for me. It was the year I crashed and burned as an alcoholic and had to do the unmentionable—ASK FOR HELP! Surprised? Below the surface of all these achievements were 13 years of progressive drinking, separations, periods of sobriety, and ultimately severe depression and suicidal ideation.

My marriage had crumbled. I had multiple accidents and injuries. I had resigned myself to never working again. I was convinced my life was over. I called an old friend, a reporter and former alcoholic who in a few hours gave me the hope that, in reality, my life was about to begin. I stopped drinking and have maintained sobriety since that night, April 13, 1972.

I have done this through association with supportive people, and by throwing myself totally into spreading the message of recovery and tirelessly helping the afflicted and affected. I have started several treatment centers and have spoken in almost every major city in Canada and the United States. After my wife had moved on (and later remarried), I spoke in Kalispell, Montana, in 1978, and that evening a beautiful woman approached me and my friends. Her marriage had also terminated through alcoholism, and she was raising three children: Craig, Carmen, and Cory. I confess I could have married her that very night. We did marry in 1982 and have had a fantastic life together. We have 18 grandchildren.

I came to learn that my father was the only male in his family who was not alcoholic. My older brother did not recover from his disease, which started in high school, and it killed him. My younger brother was a struggling artist in London, and he had become alcoholic combined with crippling bipolar disorder. I brought him to Canada, where he also found lasting sobriety. He became the renowned cartoonist GED of the *London Times, Economist, Oldie*, and other publications.

In 1987 I was made a fellow of the American College of Surgeons. I became chief of staff of my local hospital, St. Michael's, for 11 years. This was a hospital founded and operated by the Sisters of St. Martha from Nova Scotia. I have never met a group of people of such industry, dedication, professionalism, and humility in all my life, who had the courage to survive fierce political adversity. They became my dearest mentors.

Music has always been a source of great comfort. I have sung in professional concerts from the age of nine and as an adult tenor soloist in many musical theater productions.

I also became director of the new Lethbridge Cancer Center for 10 years, and it gained international recognition.

I saw people with disabilities struggling with the old folding walkers and looking for a seat to rest. I invented the very first walker with a seat, and that has become the standard around the world.

I treated many First Nations patients and was inducted a chief of the Blood Tribe in 1993. I became a Kainai Chieftain, 40 members in the world, including at the time Prince Charles and Pope John Paul II. I was named Chief Two Headdress.

After all this, what do I think success is? To me it is a passionate journey of goals and achievements. When one is accomplished, a door opens to reveal another, higher challenge. Failure is never completely out of sight.

I believe that leadership is an art you can develop. Simply, it is how you treat others. I summarize leadership like this:

> Learn from members of your team constantly.
>
> Encourage everyone—everyone counts, and they must know it.
>
> Achieve objectives with an ongoing developing plan.
>
> Don't meddle, just support.
>
> Energize others by creating a fun environment.
>
> Right people should be given the right jobs.
>
> Style is often more important than skills.

Success involves willingness to listen, to be open minded, to get involved in honest self-analysis—*awareness*. Socrates said, "The unexamined life is not worth living." Awareness will guide us to *acceptance,* which is *the key* to this inside job of peace of mind and productive change. We must "get real" and go beyond admitting problems to truly accepting and addressing them.

There is so much loud talk today about freedom. How can people be happy, joyous, and free if they are incapable of loving themselves and others (as I was, when a self-centered drunk)? How can you love in a state of anger, resentment, and fear? No, we will only love ourselves and others when we are fully *healed*. We can never heal until we have learned to *forgive* ourselves and others (the former is often the most difficult).

Gratitude is the most powerful emotion to embrace daily. An attitude of gratitude trumps all other negative feelings. Test it!

Success comes frequently through *failure* and reinvention. Always have a backup plan. *Diversify.* I have always had an insatiable appetite for knowledge outside my own field of expertise and have never boxed myself into loss of control and total dependence on others.

I could never have tackled all the above tasks without adhering very strictly to living one day at a time, in the moment. My wife, Teresa, will admonish me when I stray, saying, "Live where your feet are, Tom." Most anxieties reside in the past or the future.

What are my goals now? Well, I can't do anything personally about the Wall Street crooks who herded the masses over the precipice before safely retiring to their mansions. Small and medium-sized businesses and professionals create 50% of jobs, and I see their greatest challenge is to survive the mobile marketing tsunami. For these businesses to prosper, they will need to be re-educated to reach their customers where they are—on mobile phones and devices—by using texting, mobile websites, and social media. With 20 years' experience in online marketing, I have dedicated myself to be of help in this scary and exciting time.

In closing, I have suggested several times that you should take advice, but remember: There were three wise men, so don't depend on just one. Whatever your challenge, get started, act on it, do it now, and never utter the word "try," unless when you have the next sudden urge, you prefer to "try" to go to the toilet.

Biography

Dr. Tom Melling

DR. TOM MELLING was born in Scotland and is a retired surgeon who practiced in Scotland and Canada. He pioneered a cancer clinic, a few addiction treatment centers, and was the inventor of the first walker with a seat. He was inducted as an Indian chief twice and received many other honors. He has been a long-time  student of Internet marketing. He resides with his wife, Teresa, on Vancouver Island, Canada, and in Palm Springs.

Contact Information

drdrtom7@gmail.com
mobilemarketingcoaching.com

Chapter 6
$\mathcal{DNA}$ of Success

By Blair Dunkley

efined Natural Actions (DNA) of success came about from research that focused on language profiling, questioning skills, and behaviors of success.

Twenty-five years ago I did research followed by a series of interviews with some of the world's top billion-dollar CEOs and found they all had three things in common that led to their success. Through my teaching, this behavior pattern was duplicated in our clients and they started seeing the same success. For example, I helped one company grow from $200 million to $500 million, and another from $100,000 to $28 million in sales over a four-year period.

What I am going to share with you in this chapter is not about a happy straight line to success; but more importantly real-life accounts of survival, breakthroughs, and fire-tested tools of how to use what is innately natural to all humans; and if you know how, these Defined Natural Actions can become secret keys to your success. My story of learning to succeed, learning from others, and teaching this knowledge to others was full of unexpected challenges.

Sometimes when you're going through hell, it might seem as though you've completely moved in. I was trying to recover from financial devastation, which occurred between 2006 and 2007, after losing our family's life savings (seven figures) from the drop in the market. I had challenging decisions to make. I remember thinking things couldn't possibly get any worse. Well, I said at the time, at least we're lucky we still have our health—wrong! My wife, Melissa, was diagnosed with cancer in 2008, which was frightening and devastating for our two young girls as well as for Melissa and me. She is my partner in business as well as in life, and it hit our business hard as Melissa is a major driver behind ResultsNOW's success. So our focus in 2008 and 2009 was to get Melissa through her surgeries and back to full health again.

When Melissa returned to work, I geared up, knowing we had a full complement of coaches and trainers back, and we began to rebuild our business. However, two months after Melissa returned to work, it started with pain in my arm, neck, and chest, then severe sweats . . . you guessed it, I had an angina attack (not a full heart attack), which landed me in the hospital, immediately scheduled for a triple bypass open-heart surgery. I was totally out of the company, flat on my back, with my family worried if I would make a full recovery.

Finally, when we were finally getting our lives back on track, just days into 2010, and only 10 days after I returned to work full time, my mother, who was still running Life Skills College at the age of 87, had a stroke, and I had to step in immediately to take over her business, which had not been well managed for the past few years. This family business had created additional debt, which I was now responsible for. Once again, life had intervened with a situation I hadn't created or planned for but couldn't avoid. Boy, talk about life tests.

In these past four long years, Melissa and I have been through personal financial collapse, cancer, open-heart surgery, and my mother's stroke—do you think I could tell you a little about success and recovery? You bet! These last few years have been a deep soul-searching personal test of our own skills—skills we have taught others for decades. We knew they worked, but we'd never personally had to test them this severely. We have learned a few important lessons and had many affirmations that what we practice, the DNA skills, really works. They are fire tested, by others and by us. I found three lessons in this.

1. Be Curious

The greatest tip for success in life and in business is to be curious, curious enough to change your perspective in spite of what life may be throwing at you. Curious enough to get back up when you've been knocked down. I now look at my life, situations, people, and business, and I don't allow myself to stay stuck in only my way of seeing the world. I have expanded my perspective to include that of others, people I want to travel alongside on a journey. In doing so, we have invested in and empowered each other, creating a triple win—me, them, and an abundance of healthy situations and communities we have intentionally created together.

I have also noticed from my research and experience with clients that those who are incredibly successful tend to ask simple but highly effective questions and then listen to, not just hear, the answer.

What I found that did not work for me was to ask questions that proved my point all the time. This just fed my need to be right—sound familiar? I asked questions or made statements that got the people I was working with to agree with my position (or so I thought). I later found out, when I was more curious and open to listening, that what I was doing was not working for them. My family and friends were only telling me what they thought I wanted to hear. We'd get into arguments about whatever. You know, ego stuff. Well, they were right. I was not effective, until I got into being curious!

2. Get Out of Your Own Way

When I look back on my life, and the lives of other successful people, I see clearly that not one of us got to be successful without major mistakes and failures. Every successful person has learned to get up from their losses. You must learn from them by figuring out what worked and what didn't work and then identifying the two or three things that need to be changed. Most important of all, *make those changes.*

In putting this into practice, I noticed that I needed to get out of my own way! My need to be right, to be certain, was tripping me up. Of course everyone wants to be right, right? Well, maybe if I didn't need to be right, I could figure out what was wrong, what was not working, so I could fix it. See, I'm a guy, and I need to fix things. And this model worked well for me for several years. But what if my need to fix things was now holding me back? Mostly because I wasn't . . . you got it . . . curious.

When I stopped trying to be right, I got out of my own way. I stopped the positioning, leading questions and found increased clarity. I didn't feel the need to be certain, but I did need to find external real-world examples of what worked. This was and still is working. Examples of people who make a lot of money and have time to live a great life (such as Tim Ferris, *The 4-Hour Workweek*, and Matt Morris, *The Unemployed Millionaire*) while having great relationships (such as me) were all around. The first year I applied my own skills to my life, I went from making about $65,000 a year working full time to working only 17 weeks the very next year and making $142,000. And that was just the start.

3. Stop Judging—Start Evaluating

Before I began changing things, I judged and did not evaluate. When I started to evaluate, I noticed that I did not need to be right anymore. I needed to find what worked, what was externally verifiable. I noticed some other things as well. My confidence went up. I no longer had to do it all on my own. If I asked more effective questions and got really curious, things seemed to work out faster and with less effort. When I, for the most part, stopped judging others and myself and started evaluating, I noticed that success is all around us. Despite the odds, we can succeed.

Life Is Not Fair—And That's a Good Thing!

One of my favorite quotes is one that I found on a drink coaster: "Life guarantees a chance, NOT a fair shake." It has helped me be successful by keeping my head in the game when the rest of me wanted to give up. What if I could find a way to turn that chance into an unfair advantage? Life guarantees a chance but you have to get up and take advantage of that chance, and since this doesn't have to be fair, then what can you change in your headspace to find your unfair advantage? For me, it was language-based profiling; listening to people for a few moments then telling them all about themselves. What's yours going to be?

No matter how you measure success, you can achieve it through clarity of desired result and the ability, through practiced effective skills, to choose and execute the next steps to get where you want to be.

The single most important key in achieving success is the skill of questioning. Not just the ability to ask a question, but the mastery of questioning; to skillfully ask questions that define and clarify the root cause of a problem or challenge versus just chasing a symptom. This same skill of mastering questions applies to solving, resolving, or resourcing effective solutions to permanently change the problem and situation.

DNA Steps for Success and How to Apply Them

1. Understand your **intentions.**

2. Define your desired **result.**

3. Ask questions of yourself and others to clarify the appropriate effective **behaviors** to achieve your desired result.

4. Continually **evaluate** whether what you are doing is getting you the results you want.

I used to trust before I tried something. I would simply decide and then work at rationalizing why this was a good thing to do. This seems to be the way most people make decisions. We just make them. Learning to try, test, or compare before I decided to trust helped me take smaller steps faster, with greater clarity, by evaluating what worked and what didn't. This process helped me find key areas to change and improve. Then I would retest.

Leading Others to Success

Leadership is being able to get people to go to someplace they would not have gone on their own. In running one of my businesses, Life Skills College (we had at the peak 23 branches in Canada), I found that if I did not inspire my staff to see something they could not envision at the moment, they couldn't grow, and neither would the business. We all need to see the opportunity so that we might turn the imaginary into something real. A leader must inspire and help people to focus so that they can build their own burning desire for the vision.

This is the natural process that you are going through as you read this book. You are putting new and different information into your head so that you might be inspired to see yourself, your life situation, whatever that might be, as a unique opportunity to make a real difference in this world. It starts, as it must, in your mind, usually as a problem, sometimes as a blinding insight. No matter how it starts, it comes down to a burning desire to act. You become restless. Needing to do something, you start asking questions. It consumes your mind as your intention. You need to take action, test, and evaluate what worked and what didn't, and decide what you need to do next. Embrace this process, as it is in your DNA to succeed if you understand how to make it work for you.

Finding Mentors

Asking the right questions is important, but equally important is finding the right people to ask. Whom do you need to ask about what you might do to make this vision in your mind into something very real?

I have had many role models in my life, but my most significant was my mother and friend, Madeleine Dunkley. I am grateful to her for her support, training, and mentoring. Most people don't get a chance to work with, learn from, and be mentored by someone who was a TV personality when TV had only three channels. Madeleine forged new ground by being on *Ladies First*, a local Martha Stewart-like show, in the 1960s. She went on to find a way to take $42 million of Canadian government research and turn that into a private college in 1976 to train life skills coaches. Her ability to find a way to get something done, even when no one had done it before, was amazing. She constantly challenged others and me to look beyond the obvious and trust the process. Life guarantees a chance, but you have to take it.

Thanks, Mom.

Biography

Blair Dunkley

BLAIR DUNKLEY is the cofounder of Life Skills College and ResultsNOW. He has a 35-year reputation for owning successful training companies complemented by his lifelong investigative research to analyze and optimize behaviors for personal and corporate performance. He is a keynote speaker, trainer, corporate and executive coach, and consultant to business and organization leaders worldwide.

Contact Information

www.resultsnowinc.com
blair@resultsnowinc.com
877-600-2466
Office: 780-459-2770

Chapter 7
Succeed in Spite of the Odds

By Shirley H. Everett

*Your success depends mainly upon what you think of yourself
and whether you believe in yourself.*
—William J. H. Boetcker

*I*t was my grandma's, Gracie Waller Perkins', prayer that blessed me, my twin sister, and my loving mother to be alive today. My mother has always been a petite lady, but when my twin sister and I were born, my mother weighed less than 99 pounds and was so weak that the doctor told my grandmother that he would not be able to save both the twins and her daughter. Grandmother, who believed in the power of prayer, kneeled down by my mother's bedside and prayed this prayer: Father, bless my daughter to survive this multiple birth experience. Bless these twin girls to live also and bless me to live long enough to hear them say mommy and daddy.

Not only was my mother blessed by Grandma's prayer to birth seven more children, five boys and two more girls, but she was provided blessings for life—she lived to celebrate her 82nd birthday in April this year. Grandma lived to hear us say mommy and daddy, and she lived to attend my wedding ceremony 27 years later.

The blessings from Grandma's prayer continued with my meeting a great friend who is now my husband, Jerry. We dated for a little over a year, and Jerry was very patient with me after the proposal, because I told him I had to pray about it first and let him know when I got a sign from God. At the end of each date thereafter, he would ask me the same question: Have you gotten a sign yet? It was not very long until I got a sign of confirmation, and we planned our wedding day for June 26, 1976. On the wedding date, I was cool as a cucumber, but Jerry was so nervous that his knees were shaking as he stood in front of the congregation beside the minister and his best man, waiting for my entrance down the aisle. It was a beautiful ceremony, and one of the highlights of my life.

I live a successful life of abundance by practicing these thirteen principles.

1. Remember that all things are possible with God.
2. Live one day and one step at a time.
3. Count my blessings.
4. Take advantage of opportunities.
5. Understand the importance of overcoming negatives.
6. Prepare for success with a positive attitude.
7. Remember that visualization comes before action.
8. Know what to do and when to do it.
9. Learn from mistakes and failures.
10. Live with integrity, fairness, responsibility, trustworthiness, respect, and caring.
11. Remember that happiness is enjoyed along the way and not at the end of the journey.
12. Focus on helping others realize their dreams.
13. Have the courage to do what I know in my heart is the right thing to do.

It will take too many words to share how I have practiced all these principles in my life. Therefore I will share one example in the story that follows that will illustrate my thinking and the steps I take to ensure success as I experience life.

I begin by thinking, "A problem is an opportunity when you are one with God." When I am super confident in my abilities in some area, I will answer someone asking for my help with a resounding "No problem!" I believe this is the same thing that God answers when we ask God's help.

Have you ever been asked to perform such a simple task that you thought to yourself, No problem? You can approach every situation with this same attitude when you understand that God is your problem solver. God is ready to help you through every experience of your life. So no matter how complex or difficult some job or relationship seems to be, know that with God, all things are possible—no problem!

Growing up as a twin brought many exciting and challenging experiences. It was great to learn even as an infant that the competitive gene was part of my being. My twin sister and I were the oldest of nine siblings. My parents believed that since we came into this world together, we should stay together through all of life's experiences, including being in the same class throughout elementary and high school as well as the first four years of college.

There were lots of challenges during our elementary school experiences. During the first four years, we lived less than a block from school and could walk. It was so close that we could leave our house (running, of course) when the school bell started to ring and get to class just before the school bell stopped ringing. Before fifth grade we moved to a new house in another neighborhood but still close enough to walk to school. The principal was also the fifth-grade teacher. My sister and I were often accused of doing homework for our younger brothers. In those days, the teacher was always right. Even though we were innocent of the accusation, we had no other choice but to accept the ridicule in front of our brothers' classmates in an effort to show respect to adults. If we failed to complete an assignment during the school day, we were required to stay after school until the assignment was complete.

In the fall and winter, days were short and often it was beginning to get dark as we walked a wooded shortcut path to our home. It was a blessing that we were in the same classroom and could walk home together. Since our aunts and uncles on Dad's side of the family had built a reputation of dropping out of school at an early age for various reasons, the odds were against us to succeed. It was our fate, most thought, to become pregnant before high school. Rumors such as this seemed to haunt us from fifth grade through high school. We learned later that it was a blessing that our aunts and uncles had developed another slant to their reputation that perhaps prevented any harm from coming to us while walking home after school in fifth grade. Some said, "You had better not get the Hairston family angry with you, because they would have no problem shooting you as they looked at you." To this day it has been very confusing how this rumor developed.

Yes, growing up in a large family of nine children afforded me many experiences, such as having our own baseball team and not having to depend on the neighborhood children to cover the bases. Family Bible study and prayer time was a tradition from my mom's side of the family, and a tradition that my father took seriously. His favorite statement was "The family who prays together, stays together."

There were some exciting and positive experiences during our educational studies, because we loved learning new things. We especially loved the many ways to solve mathematical equations. I still remember clearly to this day how my sister and I would spend hours working on a problem until we found the solution. We would race home to be the first to share our experiences of the day. This is why I developed a habit of talking fast. Both of us wanted to be first to begin telling the story. Many say that they do not know how on earth one of us could begin the sentence and the other could finish it. Our parents said that this was one of our many unique qualities.

It was through the good times and the challenging times that I learned to live one day at a time and to enjoy the moment. This was the beginning of our journey recognizing how we were blessed to live abundantly in all areas of our life experiences: spiritually, socially, emotionally, physically, and financially. The following quote written by Charlene M. Proctor, Ph.D., is one of my favorites because it helps me to stay focused and grounded on the importance of enjoying success and life experiences along the way and not at the end of my journey:

> *Every day we have an opportunity to choose our attitude and focus our intentions in the present moment. We should never allow the past to hold you back from enjoying a full life. What have you got to lose, except a heavy burden? Forgiveness is usually the key to moving forward, which is why it's on the path to gaining insight. When you forgive yourself, and*

those who have hurt you, you are able to release negative patterns that visit you over and over again. More important, you will finally sever the control that a memory of another person has over you. Stay in the present, affirm the good that has been a result of a bad situation, and love your authentic self even more than you did yesterday. You can do it!

I agree with the great philosophers who say that a successful person is one who can see the best in others and does the best that he or she can. I have learned also that leaders learn. I understand that the moment I become unteachable, I lose my edge in the world. I also understand that as a leader, I must continue to find opportunities to learn, and I crave every chance to do so. I must commit to learning for the rest of my life and embrace every opportunity.

Biography

Shirley H. Everett

After 34 years of service in public education, as a kindergarten and third-grade teacher, guidance counselor, and administrator, SHIRLEY HAIRSTON EVERETT, inspirational teacher and motivational speaker, is presently working with her husband as an entrepreneur in their real estate company: Everett's Home Improvement. She  is also working in a second career as an inspirational teacher in their product service business: NGWT (N God We Trust), LLC. Her husband, Jerry, and she have developed a family board game, Living Life Abundantly, and other inspirational products to teach others how to live abundantly according to God's Prosperity Laws.

Contact Information

1239 Wildwood Road
Salem, VA 24195
540-354-5565
jean1976@comcast.net
www.blackbusinessnetwork.com/shirley
www.prosperitysigns.com

Chapter 8

Are You Successful? It's Up to You!

By Carina Kindkvist

Who Is Successful?

Are you successful if you own a multibillion-dollar company but focus only on your own gain? Are you successful if you don't pay your employees what they're worth and don't give them a chance to grow? Are you successful if you have made a lot of money but lost friendships and colleagues along the way?

I don't think so.

When I read about success, it's almost always connected to money. And to get the money, you need to have a strong desire and passion. I do not focus on money at all. I actually don't even know what I'd do if I had more money, except put more money into new projects.

When I was 20, I had a friend who dreamed about traveling. She was jealous of me because I could travel wherever I wanted. I told her I was jealous of her because of her longing to travel. It's easier to find money than to find the longing.

No one tells how much money you need to call yourself successful. It depends on who you compare yourself with. If you live in the smallest house with the cheapest car in a wealthy area, people won't see you as successful, but if you took the same house and car and moved it to a poor area, people would probably think you were successful.

If you're not focused on the money, you don't have a burning desire, and you haven't found your passion, can't you then call yourself successful?

I have no strong desire. I have no clear goal, and I haven't found my one true passion. I'm passionate about many things, and I do whatever comes my way that attracts me. I also have a need to never stop developing myself and to use what I learn.

Definition of Success

Success is a label people put on something someone has accomplished, especially if it's against all odds. It's temporary. You can have one success or be successful within one project without being successful as a person.

My first 15 years, I lived in a small village. Most of my classmates did not go to high school. I did. I moved to my own apartment when I was 15. I studied one year at university, and I was really successful.

Then, when I moved to Stockholm, most of my colleagues had university degrees. I was told that without a Ph.D. I could forget a career. Then, I did not feel successful.

To be successful is something more sustainable and involves the whole picture.

Lars had a franchise company for 26 years. Almost every year he was number one in sales. He was successful, and he lived like a king. Then he was forced into bankruptcy because of problems with the franchisor. Today Lars lives in a trailer. He can't start a company because of his debts, and no company wants to hire him because of his age. But he accepts the situation and makes the best of it. He never complains, doesn't blame anyone else, and has no hunger for revenge. Is he successful?

The Swedish word for success is *framgång*, which literally means walking forward. The word for successful is *framgångsrik,* which can be translated as walking plenty ahead (*gå rikligt framåt).* If you take big leaps in your development, you are successful.

Am I Successful?

I run a successful company. I live in a big house in one of the most attractive areas in Sweden. I have great friends, a wonderful family, and fantastic employees. I haven't taken any medication for 14 years.

Earlier I didn't think I was successful.

I had excuses for everything. I could have a more beautiful house, a more successful company, and so on. And most of my success I referred to as plain luck.

The problem was I didn't know what success was to me. I bothered too much about others' definitions of success and became a victim of how I thought others wanted me to live.

My Definition of Being Successful

To be successful is most of all a question of attitude. Everybody has to define their own definition of success. For me the key is to decide that I am successful right now and to just continue to show, improve, and prove I am successful to myself.

My definition is based on my values.

- To develop and to help people around me develop

- To be passionate about what I do

- To be happy with my environment (where I live, my body, my family, colleagues, and friends)

- To be financially independent and choose to work when I want.

Seven Tips for Success and How I Apply Them

1. Watch Out for the Rat Race

When I think about success, money is involved to a certain extent. I don't think you can call yourself successful if you don't have money to buy food. But who decides how much money you need to be successful?

Only you can do that.

It's easier to be financially independent if your costs are low. I'm thankful to my parents who raised me not to buy anything before I actually had the money. I have low costs of living, and my passive income streams cover my monthly bills and expenses. I'm free not to work if I don't want to.

2. Seek a Good Portion of Luck (or Positive Affirmation)

I have a good portion of luck, and the more I say I'm lucky, the luckier I get. It is a successful self-fulfilling prophecy.

Of all the impressions I am bombarded with, most are neutral, some show I'm lucky, and others that I'm unlucky. I choose to look out for signals that confirm I'm lucky.

I needed a jack and suddenly I passed a shop where there was a sale on jacks. My usual luck, I thought. How often is there a sale on jacks? But I couldn't see any jacks close to the sale sign in the shop. I asked a shop assistant, who said, "No, if there aren't any here, they are sold out." I had such good luck to find them on sale, but such bad luck that they were sold out.

I walked up to the cashier and asked again. "I think we might have a few more in store." And of course, there they were. I'm lucky as usual.

When I was in India, we coined the phrase "Tick the universe, and wait for delivery." My Indian friends are convinced that when we are clear in our communication, we attract what we want. I agree.

3. Don't Bother with What Other People Think

The years 1997–2000 I took a lot of evening classes in personal development. This period changed my life. The classes really helped me to see myself and the world in a better way. The training company didn't advertise at all; instead they inspired (some say forced) the participants to tell their friends about how great it was.

I was excited and wanted all my friends to experience the change I had experienced. But the training company got a bad reputation, and my friends truly believed I was caught in a cult.

This was the first time ever I really took a stand, although it was uncomfortable. This gave me an important strength—to stand for what I believe in and not let opinions (based on lack of knowledge) destroy me.

4. Cultivate Supportive Relationships

If you want to be successful, it helps to stay away from people who hold you down. Some people don't want you to do things they don't dare, and they want you to stay as you are.

Two of my friends never said anything positive, found plenty of mistakes with me, and disagreed with everything I said. I told them this really made me sad and that I wanted them to change that behavior. Then one of them told me I wasn't her favorite. The other told me she was still concerned that "I was involved in a cult." They had an "I don't like you" and a "cult" filter when they talked and listened to me.

It was easy to see why I felt like a failure with them. I realized that in that kind of environment, it's hard to feel successful.

5. Accept Your Body

Can you be fat and successful at the same time? Yes, if you accept your weight and if you are happy with your body. I was 15 kilograms obese for many years. I didn't like to read about all the consequences my BMI could have on my health. And I couldn't dress in line with my picture of a successful business woman. I was always on a diet, which really destroyed my self-confidence. I felt that all the success in my life was worthless when I was of such a weak nature that I couldn't control my weight.

The turning moment came when I went to Overeaters Anonymous and realized I was a sugar addict. I have a "sugar addict gene" in my brain similar to people who are dyslexic. When I witnessed former alcoholics and drug addicts saying that the sugar addiction was way more heavy to handle, I finally realized my weight had nothing to do with whether I was successful or not. It was actually not my fault.

6. Have a Great Leader or Be Your Own

An important part of your environment is your manager. It's much easier to be successful if your manager sees you as successful.

I coached a very skilled and talented guy. The problem was that his boss only appreciated social skills. After constant pressure to become more social, my client's confidence had dropped. He found a new job where the new boss could see his strengths. Today he is successful in his new occupation.

A leader needs to see that every person is unique. The leader needs to believe in the people she leads. If the leader has just a little doubt about an employee, she stands in the way of the success of the employee.

7. Find Your Talents

My favorite quote on success is "Success is not to be a copy of someone else, it is to be a first class version of yourself" (Jonas Ridderstråle). If you copy someone else, you will never use all your true talents. If you become more of yourself, you will end up using your true potential.

When you use your full potential, you are successful.

Biography
Carina Kindkvist

After a career in the IT field, CARINA KINDKVIST switched paths and founded the Coach House as the first Nordic coach broker company in 2002. Carina is an inspirational speaker and a certified coach. She was ICF Nordic President in 2008 and is often referred to as the coaching mom of Sweden. Carina is a true entrepreneur  and engages in the board for the National Association of Small Entrepreneurs. She also runs a conference center for entrepreneurs in the middle of Stockholm.

Contact Information

CoachHuset i Skandinavien AB
Luntmakargatan 52
Stockholm, Sweden
+46 8 333 131
info@coachhuset.com
www.coachhuset.com
www.motesrum.com
www.lifeville.se

Chapter 9

Your Voice. Your Message. Your World.

By Lewis S. Lewis

Because of this book, *The Art & Science of Success*, I began to reflect on how I'd come to this point in my life and where I'd be heading from here. That's when it dawned on me that my childhood held part of the key that brought me to where I am today and where I plan to be tomorrow.

We love our children, and we want them to succeed in life, so expose them to as much as you possibly can as often as you possibly can. Provide them guidance and encourage them. Allow them to make mistakes, pick them up, dust them off, and encourage them to continue. Praise their efforts and encourage them even more. Assure them that they will do great things as they grow older. Make it a point to do so every day.

On with my story:

The stage had been set, the curtains were drawn, and a new era in communications lay just out of sight. What stood ever present and directly before me was a seemingly insurmountable monster, a formidable foe I had avoided at all costs my entire adult life.

Known by many, to a lesser extent I'm sure, this monster would be no match for me this day. I grinned as I thought, "Either get past this challenge and put into motion what I've worked so hard for, or fold like a lawn chair and go home." No doubt, a no-brainer, and still my heart was beating a thousand times a second as I peered about the audience. I reminded myself, "This is less about me and more about them." The emcee continued my introduction.

Earlier in the day I had walked the set, taking into account the size of the stage on which I would make my stand. It was at least 50 feet across in my mind's eye. The rows of chairs set to accommodate the audience were impressive and daunting by any standard.

Up until now the thought of speaking to a group, and even the thought of standing in front of a video camera for that matter, was a terrifying proposition, let alone standing center stage with a live audience. The difference now was that the tides had turned, and having the ability to communicate to others from the stage was of paramount importance to me. Little did anyone know, it was of paramount importance to almost everyone.

With my back against the wall, I stood in anxious anticipation of this inaugural event. Slowly but surely the last few seconds prior to facing this beast steadily dwindled.

Early on I came to the realization that this step would be just one of many defining moments that lay ahead of me. It was never really a matter of whether I would proceed. It was more of a matter of cornering myself intentionally and then rising to the occasion.

Seemingly within an instant, the anticipated moment had arrived. It was as if I were a new recruit again being ushered off the bus at boot camp. Just as I could hear the drill sergeants outside yelling, "Go, go, go!" I remember being caught up in the mass stampede that ensued to please them. It was now go time once again, as the emcee announced to the audience, "So, please put your hands together and give a warm welcome to Lewis Lewis, the man so nice they named him twice!"

I entered the stage from the left to greet the young man who had made my introduction. We promptly shook hands, and I accepted my position behind the lectern. As he exited I took one deep breath to settle myself. I began by acknowledging the audience, using an even cadence I had practiced again and again: "Hello, ladies and gentlemen, my name is Lewis Scott Lewis."

Then in one fluid motion I darted out from behind the lectern to my left, literally running sideways, then paused briefly after three long strides, throwing my hands into the air as if I were hanging a placard with my name emblazoned on it, and excitedly exclaiming, "Lewis!" Picking up where I'd left off, I continued my dash toward center stage, stopping suddenly to again press my hands into the air, shouting, "Scott!" Again gaining my stride I continued across the stage until coming to a screeching halt just short of the opposite end. I voiced loudly with both arms reaching up to the heavens, "Lewis!"

There was a momentary pause, so silent it could have revealed the sound of a cricket coming from the back of the auditorium had I wavered a nanosecond longer, and I began to speak: "As you can see, I have a really big name. But wait! There's more!"

I began running again. But this time I was running to my right and pausing to reiterate my last, middle, and first name while once again throwing up my hands into the air just as I had done moments before. I stopped much closer to center this time, and when I came to rest, I exclaimed, "You see, it's a fun name too! You can say it forwards and backwards and you still end up with me."

My first snicker from the audience was at hand, and my ice breaker had worked superbly. This in itself was a success unlike any other I'd ever experienced in my lifetime. There I stood, liberated, undaunted, and ready to be accepted for what I had to share. A part of me.

To understand and fully take advantage of the art and science of success, one might seek third-party resources that are designed to help us overcome seemingly impossible challenges. Contracting professional assistance for coaching, training, marketing, and other resources to assist us past these challenges is, luckily for us, much more accessible than ever before.

It was out of necessity and a drive to succeed in getting my unique message out to the world that I went online and began to research public speaking. I searched for a nationally known organization, Toastmasters, which assisted with public speaking, and I readily discovered a meeting place within a mile from my home.

Not only did I find a local resource, I've acquired new friends who share a similar interest in overcoming the challenges they face in perfecting the art of speaking to live audiences. Most importantly, Toastmasters has enabled me to see beyond the fear of public speaking, seek out and appreciate professional one-on-one coaching, and practice to improve a skill set that I had once thought to be completely unattainable. This in itself has been a personal success in my life, but wait, there's more!

Back on stage I began to explain that I was often asked why my parents named me Lewis Lewis. Since I myself had the same question during my childhood, I shared with the audience one of the answers I had been given.

"After a tussle at the playground," I explained, "I remember coming home and asking Mom why she named me Lewis Lewis. Without hesitation she looked me square in the eyes with as big a smile as she could muster and said "Scott." She always called me Scott. "Scott, your name is going to prove to be great for sales!" She paused for a moment to let that sink in, then continued. "People are going to remember you! Be sure to tell them what you know!"

I thought, Wow! I do know a little bit about sales, and I am eight and a half years old now! As I stood there, looking skyward with my hands on my hips, my mind began to race over the new direction and encouragement I'd been given. And since it sounded like a lot of fun, and my mother was obviously excited about it, I couldn't wait to get started.

Note: I'd like to stop there and ask you to imagine how important this type of encouragement could be to a young child you know. I'd also like you to remember how important it was or would have been had you received a similar message.

I went on to complete my presentation, and in the end I received high marks during the critique of my performance. By no stretch of the imagination do I believe I'm an expert practitioner of this art; however, I am confident that I will not crumble when the time comes to take the stage again, and that, my friends, is a huge success in and of itself.

I was that kid with a lemonade stand set up in front of his house, selling glasses of ice cold lemonade for 15 cents and tumblers for 25 cents to passersby and loving every minute of it. I soon graduated to picking up golf balls along the side of a local golf course and selling them back to the pro shop.

I didn't stop there. Like most kids, I'd buy comic books, but I bought them less for their stories and more so I could read the classified ads they contained. What I didn't understand was why everybody wasn't running around with x-ray glasses, dropping stink bombs, and shaking hands with a buzzer in their palm that to this day still gives me the willies every time I think about it.

I'd studied my father's *Popular Mechanics* and *Popular Science* classifieds cover to cover, wondering how I would word my own sales copy (before I knew what it was called) if I had something of value to offer adults. I'm still a kid in that sense.

Barring my nine years of service in the U.S. Army as a communications expert and air traffic control supervisor, I have always enjoyed sales; however, marketing and assisting others to achieve the successes they seek in life have become my true passions.

Imagine now a world where you can represent yourself and your city and stand out in a global crowd. Where you can become part of a new revolution in the way writers, musicians, entertainers, businesses, and professionals are paired with quality-conscious readers and consumers interested specifically in what you have to share. I'm happy to announce that now you may go to www.TweetMeWorld.com and take advantage of my passion to assist you in your success. Come join us as we celebrate—Your Voice. Your Message. Your World.™

Biography

Lewis S. Lewis

LEWIS S. LEWIS is an entrepreneur, a philanthropist, a world-class marketing innovator, and a global media visionary. With his launch of www.TweetMeWorld.com in 2011, Lewis presented the world with a new paradigm in communications both online and off that pairs local city writers, musicians, entertainers, businesses, and busi-ness professionals with quality-conscious readers and consumers worldwide. Lewis represents San Diego, California, as his home and invites you to join in representing your city and what you have to offer.

Contact Information

4364 Bonita Road
Bonita, CA 91902
619-254-2763
MyStory@TweetMeWorld.com | @LewisSLewis

Chapter 10

How Anyone Can Beat the #1 Cause of Failure

By Denis Murdock

W hen *Fortune* magazine asked Bill Gates to explain the astounding success of his brainchild, Microsoft, his immediate response was, *"Our vision, which has not changed since the day the company was founded."*

When looking at an acorn, most people see the fruit of an oak tree. Visionaries like Bill Gates see a tree . . . a forest . . . a city . . . a nation. What do you see?

What I have learned from my own personal successes and failures, my professional experience coaching 15,000 clients seeking new employment or self-employment, and my close observation of highly successful people, is that the *#1 cause of failure is Myopia.*

Yes, most who fail to succeed suffer from Myopia: the lack of foresight or discernment; small-mindedness; nearsightedness; shortsightedness; inability to see into the future; lack of purpose, intention, or vision.

My greatest accomplishments began with a desire and an intention to achieve the best possible outcome (sometimes to avoid an unwanted outcome). This was nourished by laser focusing on a definite purpose, knowing precisely what I wanted and why, and a consuming obsession for its achievement (often going without sleep or meals for days at a time). Conversely, hindsight reveals that my failures resulted from Myopia.

80% Myopically Misemployed

According to Dr. Herbert M. Greenberg, president, Marketing Survey and Research Corporation, *"80% of the work force in the U.S. is misemployed. People often stumble into jobs because of a newspaper advertisement, a previous summer job, because a friend tells them it's in a lucrative field, or some other accident. Few overcome their beginning."*

Dr. Greenberg's comment does not come as a surprise to most. Surveys indicate that 80% of the working population is dissatisfied with their current employment. They would not hesitate to change jobs if they knew what other options were available. On some level, they know they are misemployed— mismatched to their job, a square peg in a round hole.

Everything Falls into Place Once You Are Focused

During my 15 years' experience coaching, I discovered that 80–90% of my clients were not focused. When I asked job seekers what kind of job they wanted, the typical response was, *"I need a good job that pays well . . . more security . . . growth potential . . . medical benefits . . . retirement benefits."* Those interested in self-employment wanted out of the mainstream, believing that to be self-employed would provide more security than being subject to layoffs, or they desired to make more money with greater independence and autonomy.

Always I asked clients what they would do if I gave them a magic wand, without any conditions or restrictions. They usually answered, *"Wow, I don't really know. I never thought about it."* Most saw only immediate, urgent needs, not knowing what they wanted to do.

When clients seeking new jobs focused on what they wanted, interviews and job offers began to flow much more easily and more often. Financing, business partners, and clients began to manifest after my self-employed clients were focused enough to develop a concise business plan. Everything began to fall magically into place when they became focused.

You Can't Improve What You Don't Measure

Circle the number below that best represents your agreement with the following statement.

Focus Statement 1—I have a definite desire and intention to achieve the best possible outcome (or to avoid an unwanted outcome); I am laser focused on a definite purpose; I know precisely what I want, and why it is important to me, and I have a consuming obsession for its achievement.

Focus Score 1

Totally Disagree				Somewhat Agree				Totally Agree	
1	2	3	4	5	6	7	8	9	1 0

How Long Can You Tread Water?

Assuming the water in the swimming pool is comfortable, how long can you tread water? One minute? Five minutes? Ten minutes? Twenty minutes? One hour? Several hours? Write down your answer on a piece of paper. If you will increase by ten times the length of time that you wrote down, I will offer you a million dollars. Now how long can you tread water? All things are possible to those with a vision.

What the mind of man can conceive and believe, it can achieve.
—Napoleon Hill

How to Improve Your Field and Depth of Vision

Can you envision a faster, safer, higher quality, less expensive, more effective, more efficient mousetrap . . . paper clip . . . safety pin . . . pencil . . . pen . . . toothpaste . . . teeth whitener . . . eye glasses . . . way to grow hair . . . way to remove hair . . . food storage . . . recipe or cookbook . . . clothing design . . . building material . . . automobile . . . airplane . . . boat . . . fuel . . . energy . . . anti-aging treatment . . . nutritional supplement . . . weight loss system . . . pain reliever . . . cancer or diabetes cure . . . social, entertainment, or training media . . . advertising slogan . . . money-making system . . . marketing, public relations, political, or economic strategy? Whenever you get an idea for something that could be improved or invented, write it down while it is fresh on your mind for future reference.

Losers Think Short Term . . . Winners Think Long Term

Most people tend to focus on immediate pleasure and urgent demands, confusing activity with accomplishment. They choose *American Idol* or *Dancing with the Stars* over planning their next career move or business strategy. They prefer socializing at happy hour or on Facebook rather than envisioning their future with incredibly rewarding outcomes.

Losers always think short term; they contemplate the next step . . . then see what happens from there. Winners think strategically toward the long term; they begin at the end . . . then plan backwards.

Predict the Future

The good news is you no longer need to leave your life to chance, fate, or luck. In fact, you can predict your future, because you can create your future. If you desire to become laser focused, define what you want and why, and improve your field and depth of vision, fasten your seatbelt for the ride of your life! You will learn how to beat the #1 cause of failure, increase your confidence and enthusiasm, turbo charge your successes 100% . . . and more!

1. What Is Your Ultimate End of Life Outcome?

What if you had a magic wand; what if you were to dream and allow your creative imagination to run wild; what if there were absolutely no obstacles, restrictions, or conditions; what would you want to be, do, or have before you die? Write all of your ideas down on your Dream Sheet, or Bucket List, before you kick the bucket. Remember, anything and everything is possible. Keep adding to this list as you get new ideas in the future.

2. Why Is It Important?

Steve Jobs said, *"We never focus on the 'How,' only the 'Why.'"* When you know what you want, and why it is important to you, you will more easily determine how to achieve the results you seek. Everything falls into place once you are focused; when the "What" and "Why" are strong enough, the "How" will manifest itself. Now, next to each item on your Dream Sheet, or Bucket List, write down why each one is so important to you.

3. What Are the Obstacles?

If Murphy's Law runs true, things will always get in the way. Life has a way of blocking our efforts to begin or finish a project and get what we want. What are those obstacles, restrictions, or conditions that are preventing you from manifesting your dreams right now in the present moment, or in the immediate future? For example, if you want to start up or purchase an existing business, or expand your existing business, one of your obstacles might be that you do not have enough startup or working capital.

4. What Is Your Best Approach?

Considering the obstacles, should you go over the hill, under the hill, around the hill, or through the hill? Whatever you do, do something; don't just stare at the hill! There are numerous possibilities for overcoming each obstacle. Consider what strategic (long-term) and tactical (short-term) approaches are your best bets. Continuing with the previous example of lack of capital, you might consider any or all of the following possibilities: (1) get an unsecured loan or a line of credit from a financial institution; (2) get a letter of credit from a financial institution; (3) secure a loan or line of credit from a financial institution using accounts receivable, durable goods, home equity, machinery, or other equipment; (4) acquire new credit cards; (5) increase the balance on existing credit cards; (6) factor accounts receivable; (7) borrow from family and/or friends; (8) provide a public stock offering; (9) provide a private stock offering; (10) find an investor or financial partner; (11) use venture capital; (12) bootstrap; (13) sell your business and become an intrapreneur; (14) merge your business with a competitor or compatible business; (15) sell off a product line, department, or division of your company; (16) get lines of credit or extended terms with creditors and vendors; (17) secure up-front deposits of cash from clients/customers.

5. What Is Your Next Step?

To climb a ladder or stairs, you begin with step one, two, three, and so on, until you reach the top. As you read this, you may be well on your way, or just starting. Considering your best strategic and tactical approaches, what are your next steps, the most urgent and important tasks? You might select the easiest one to get the momentum started, because you know that success builds confidence. Continuing with the previous example of lack of capital, you might consider that with a single phone call and application over the phone (killing two birds with one stone), you could (1) acquire an additional credit card, and (2) increase the balance on an existing credit card.

Measure . . . Measure

Let's measure once again to see if you have made any progress thus far. Circle the number below that best represents your agreement with the following statement.

Focus Statement 2—I have a definite desire and intention to achieve the best possible outcome (or to avoid an unwanted outcome); I am laser focused on a definite purpose; I know precisely what I want, and why it is important to me, and I have a consuming obsession for its achievement.

Focus Score 2

Totally Disagree				Somewhat Agree				Totally Agree	
1	2	3	4	5	6	7	8	9	1 0

Focus Score 1: _____.(1)

Focus Score 2: _____.(2)

My **Focus Score** improved by (subtract line [1] from line [2]): _____.(3)

If your **Focus Score** improved, then line (3) above is 1 or more. Congratulations, you are off to a great start!

We Become What We Think About

Earl Nightingale said, *"The key to success and the key to failure is this: we become what we think about."* Increase your **Focus Score** even more by thinking about **Your Ultimate End of Life Outcome**, **Why It Is Important**, the **Obstacles**, the **Best Approach**, and the **Next Step**. Review your Dream Sheet, or Bucket List, each morning and evening. Place reminders on 4" × 6" cards in several conspicuous places so you will think of them several times per day: makeup or shaving mirror, refrigerator, car dashboard, desk, and computer screen at home and work.

Transmute Focus into Vision and Consuming Obsession

Continue to increase your **Focus Score** by stimulating your creative imagination to acquire a vision of your potential, what you can become and achieve. Read books; attend seminars, workshops, and lectures; listen to CDs; study the experts in your chosen field of endeavor; find a mentor or coach and become an apprentice; join or form a mastermind group; study and observe those who have already achieved what you are seeking to achieve; seek opportunities to network and surround yourself with like-minded, successful people.

How much time and money are you willing to invest in yourself to get your **Focus Score** to a level 10 and manifest your consuming obsession? The investment in your education and training in the "University of Success" will provide you the greatest return of any investment you will ever make.

Complimentary Focusing Exercises

If you would like to increase your **Focus Score**, email me your request with *Complimentary Focusing Exercises* in the subject line, and you will receive the following four exercises within 24 hours.

1. Core Competencies
2. Core Interests

3. Core Values

4. Option-Value Matrix

If you have questions or feedback, I would love to hear from you.

Biography

Denis Murdock

DENIS MURDOCK cherishes his 40 years as entrepreneur and consultant to small business, coaching 15,000 clients seeking new employment and self-employment. This is complemented by 20 years as an officer in the U.S. Army Reserves. He is the author of *The Job Seeker's Bible—How to Create Your Dream Job and Get It*, available  at Amazon.com, and has been listed in *Who's Who Worldwide*, *Who's Who in America*, *Who's Who in the West*, and *Who's Who in Sales and Marketing*.

Contact Information

4881 Denaro Drive
Las Vegas, NV 89135
702-575-5086
murdockgroup@earthlink.net
www.dreamjobsusa.com/yourwishisyourcommand

Chapter 11

Achieve Stratospheric Success through Influence

By Selva Sugunendran

*E*veryone dreams of being successful, and many reach a form of success one way or another throughout life. You can excel and even become great in many areas, such as in your career, financial status, family life, sports, physical fitness, relationships, and so on. Self-motivation and determination are essential to success no matter how you define it, but the fuel that will launch you to new heights of stratospheric success is influence.

The ability to influence others is not about pressuring or manipulating others to do what you want. Just the opposite. Genuine influence stems from putting others first. When you help them achieve their dreams, they help you go beyond even your highest expectations—not because they have to, but because they *want* to.

The Basics of Success

Success is basically reaching your potential by overcoming challenges. This can apply to different aspects of your life, depending on your goals. You need to set goals and objectives first to identify whether you've reached new heights and to provide direction for your efforts. These goals should target a range of areas based largely on your current strengths and weaknesses.

Give your weaknesses extra time and prioritize improving them as much as possible so you can quickly cope with the requirements of being successful and achieve higher forms of success. Keep in mind, however, that setting goals to improve your strengths is just as crucial as working on your weaknesses. When you master what you're already good at, not only are you able to take your success to a new level, you are better able to use your expertise to help others, which in turn helps you soar even higher. Stratospheric success means achieving more than the average person, expanding beyond your current capabilities and doing more than what is expected.

The Law of Influence

Stratospheric success goes hand in hand with the law of influence. Your influence will be determined by how much more you value other people's interests first. This selflessness is key in achieving your own goals and moving forward toward huge and nonstop success.

People generally like to work with and help individuals whom they trust and who supported them in the past. Emphasizing the interests of other people first means adding value to each person and helping them all gain newfound insight and skills throughout life. As a result, you will be leading able and strong individuals who can push you to new heights and expand your limits.

This approach might sound like the opposite of what you're planning. You might be wondering how you can achieve on your own if you prioritize others first. As the saying goes, however, "A chain is only as strong as its weakest link." If you fail to help another reach his potential or work on his weaknesses, the time will come when you will be hindered because of that person's limitation, regardless of how skillful and knowledgeable you are.

Understanding Priorities

Your own success, and the success of others, depends on understanding how and what to prioritize. If you don't devote your time and energy to what matters most, you can work hard and still end up with little to show for it but a string of small successes that leave you feeling unfulfilled.

Prioritize your goals according to what you need most in your life, but keep in mind that you won't reach the stratosphere overnight. Most of us would like to accomplish big tasks first, but if you take on too much, you are likely to end up frustrated. Break down your big dreams into smaller and more practically accomplished objectives.

Certain goals have requisites—not only to be able to achieve them but to be capable of sustaining the success once you have it. You won't be able to reach these goals or hold on to success without first learning from your previous accomplishments. What do you need to work on? What do you need in your life right now? What aspects do you need to change to reach a particular goal? These questions will help you prioritize better and achieve success in what matters most to you.

Prioritizing other people will help you reach stratospheric success. As a leader, understanding the needs and potential of your people helps you guide them to work on the most important areas in their lives and find new ways to bring them closer to their goals. Putting the needs of others above yours will render extraordinary results that one individual cannot achieve properly. You will get a lot of help and speed up whatever you are trying to achieve as soon as you guide others to accomplish their current objectives and address issues that hinder their progress and yours. Whether you are working for another company or running your own business, your success depends on your ability to lead yourself and others.

Becoming a Leader

Successful leaders consider the welfare of the entire team, and they understand that their own success includes the achievements of others. Leadership encompasses self-worth and confidence—being able to lead yourself and set an example as well as ignite others to work better and to become better people. Others quickly recognize when leaders focus on everyone else's particular needs and interests and thus will work harder and give more to reap the rewards.

One form of leadership that will strengthen your influence is coaching. In the process of coaching others to make better decisions, you also discover more about yourself. Being a coach puts you at the forefront of the action. Having people by your side, especially those who have become knowledgeable and skilled due to your help, will bring you to your own goals faster, with permanent results.

Strengthening Your Independence

To lead yourself, and therefore to be able to lead others, requires a great deal of independence. Independence means having the capacity to create goals and achieve them using your own skills, knowledge, and personal strengths. Your level of independence will be based on your experience and how much you trust yourself in achieving the objectives you make in life. However, you will also need to have a solid support system and particular roles in other people's endeavors. The relationship becomes two way, mutually achieving goals and meeting the needs of all in the process.

This does not mean that influence deviates from independence. You have to be a master of yourself first before you can motivate others and lead them to reach personal growth and success. You won't be able to give them support and insight into honing their skills or identifying and solving problems if you do not know how to conquer yourself first. Having the right background is essential, since every person's situation is different. Responses to your leadership will vary, and hence influence will be a huge motivator in helping people make the right choices.

Your Influencing Skills

So how exactly do you go about honing your influence? There is no universal way to influence others. There are no formulas or set guidelines, since each person has unique skills, experience, and responses. However, you can start understanding every individual by assessing his potential and knowing more about his personal goals and objectives. You can gauge the person's strong and weak areas, then devise a plan for how you can put his interests first and help him prioritize the areas that need the most work.

In the workplace, this means establishing trust and building rapport with your people, inspiring them when they make small accomplishments or become active in the group, letting them know about their strengths and weaknesses, pushing their imagination, helping them forge new relationships, building leadership, enforcing discipline, and leading by example.

Influencing others means having the right words to say, being encouraging and rewarding them. Long-term benefits (or rewards) become available once they start working toward their goals. They will experience positive results by doing things differently or facing the challenge instead of waiting for someone else to take over or being passive about everything else going on around them. If you influence them positively, your job gets easier, since you will have active and helpful members working with you.

To excel at influencing others, you will need to mix your skills in presentation, assessment, interpersonal techniques, communication, assertiveness, perseverance, and attention to detail combined with a big picture perspective. You have to teach your people how to develop these skills too. Behavior and attitude have a lot to do with how each person will respond and face the challenges in his life.

Positive Influence

Nowadays, most experts agree that positive influence or reinforcement is key in helping people realize their potential. Traditional methods of manipulation, coercion, and force do not have long-term positive effects and can create rifts and compromised relationships. It is often unhealthy to force people against their will. They might function for a time, but often only when you're present. Trust cannot be built this way, and you will have to put in more time and effort just to make sure they're contributing to the team.

Positive influence encourages people to work independently and put others' interests first and include you in their priorities. People generally remember good experiences, and if they see you as a good motivator and influencer, you will benefit more as they expand your network and work hard to bring you closer to your goal.

Communication

Humans are generally motivated or encouraged for their own reasons and benefits, not yours. They need a mentor or an educator with whom they can easily talk about their fears, goals, desires, experiences, and challenges. Clear communication is a useful tool if you want to be valued, approved of, and respected. What you say is important, but more crucial is what you hear. You need to listen carefully to the interests and needs of your people so that you can help them achieve their dreams, which in turn will lift you closer to your own.

Self-Awareness

Before you begin influencing other people, you have to be aware of yourself. All great leaders and communicators are self-aware. Even though you put others' interests and needs before yours, you should still be completely aware of your own needs, strengths, and limitations. Understanding your limitations will help when coaching others.

The combination of self-awareness and awareness of others means not forcing them to respond the same way you react to your personal experiences. In reaching stratospheric success, you can either influence or be influenced. If you lack self-awareness, there's a big chance that others will persuade you instead of the other way around.

Valuing Others

One of the most important laws of stratospheric success is understanding the value of giving more than you pay for. This means that you understand how to make payments and offer more at first, knowing that the rewards will be greater in the end. This coincides very well with the need to put the interests of others first to experience great success for yourself in the end. The more value you put in other people, the more value you get in return. The value you create in other people will be more than the value you can generate working alone.

Value is created when you teach them the right values, attitude, and activities that will improve their self-worth and motivate them to give their best in every endeavor. Help people realize their potential and understand their own strengths and weaknesses. Show them why you value them and they will give you far more than you "pay" for in your time and effort.

A Lifetime of Increasing Success

Focusing on strengths and helping others enjoy the rewards will provide you with endless benefits for years to come. Connecting with people develops your network, so you can also find other successful people whose role is to help you realize your aspirations and push you to do better each time. You will find other leaders whose need is to develop your interests. You will feel the same need to achieve and exert all your efforts so you can reach your goals and support them in reaching theirs. You will develop the utmost respect for these great mentors and educators, and you will pass on what you learn to the people you mentor and teach.

The more successful others are, the more successful you are. The higher you soar, the better your perspective on what it takes to fly even higher. Once you reach the stratosphere, there's no place to go but up.

Biography

Selva Sugunendran

SELVA SUGUNENDRAN worked for major UK organizations, including GEC, Plessey, Racal, EMI, and Thorn, often in senior management positions. In 1985, he formed his own IT company. His software was installed in major blue chip companies, including BMW, Rolls Royce, Virgin Atlantic HQ, Lloyds of London, and Ministry of Defence sites.

Since selling his last company, he has worked as a consultant in Integrated Business Solutions as well as in many online ventures. Selva has written several eBooks and articles on Internet marketing, social media marketing, personal empowerment, and Health, Wealth & Success. He also supports charitable organizations protecting the very young from abuse and helping the very old to live with dignity. You can find him on Facebook, Twitter, Linked-In, YouTube, and ezinearticles.com.

Contact Information

selva@SuccessWithoutLimits.biz
www.blog.SuccessWithoutLimits.biz
www.empowerment.SuccessWithoutLimits.biz
www.health.SuccessWithoutLimits.biz

Chapter 12

The Word Impossible with a Tweak and You've Got Your Success

By Arthur Taubo

*I*n the entrance on the way to my office, there is an old bookbinder press, once used to make the perfect shape of a book. Within that press is a book written in Latin, dated 1516. It has been owned by many, and during the last few decades by my family. None of my visitors takes any notice of this book. It does not scream out. It just lies there, vulnerable, waiting, without feelings of world events, honorable mentions, or praise. The printer who created it I know nothing about, and most likely no one else knows who he was or how life was treating him. But in his time, he was a Master and authority on a valuable subject of great interest. The Master has been dead for more than four hundred years, but the elaborately designed book is this very moment in my hands.

Larger Than Me—With a Flip It Becomes We

Success is for me something far greater than the abundance of money and results achieved right here and now. As a human being of flesh and blood on a planet in an infinite universe, I cannot help but to think big when I think of success. And in doing so, I put my effort in thinking—time, space, and beyond—with the end goal in mind. I'm asking myself the following question:

How should I best manage my precious time here on earth so that people, beyond my departure, can enjoy what I added, without my selfishness and importance in mind? For I have come to realize that success is not about me. Success is beyond me. Success is about us—you and me, we the people. It's about those who have lived before us, we who are alive, and those who run the next leg of the relay.

So What Is Success, Who Has It, And How Does One Achieve It?

I hope you don't mind what I'm about to tell you, but if you do, there is not much I can do about it since it took place several years ago. Back then I had a studio in downtown Oslo where I painted oil paintings. I spent most of the daytime outside, beside a lake on the island where I grew up. That's where I sketched and reflected during a two-year period. I reflected over beauty, potential, capabilities, and success. Back in the studio, resting in an old green chair next to the easel, I ended up jotting down the following sentence:

"You are a tulip even if you are an onion left in the dark underground!"

When I think back on this sentence, something strikes me: You and I are unique and valuable living creatures despite our achievements. We are the only "us" in the history of mankind. And that, my friend, is nothing less than a miracle. We are perfectly designed and created to be who we really are. The great thing is that it actually took place before we were born. Before we had our own consciousness. Before we started to evaluate and compare ourselves with others. I'm not sure if anyone has told you what I'm going to tell you right now: You are a success.

You have always been a success, and you are here for a specific reason: to get your talent and passion off the ground and into the world. And as we speak, this very moment, there are people waiting for you to stretch up and into the air. There are millions out there who need to hear the message you have within. The old guy at the corner needs to hear those words from you. That old friend you haven't seen in years would enjoy your call today. While you think about who that person might be, I'd like to ask you a few questions. If everything were possible, and you could choose whatever you wanted, what would that be? What is the first thing that comes to mind?

Is it something that makes you smile and feel happy inside? Does it include other people? Is it something you have been thinking of but not yet done? Is there a person that you should forgive? Is it something that you can imagine that you are doing? How is it to be where you see yourself? Looking back from that point, what have you accomplished? Are you glad you did it? Are the people around you glad you did what you have done? When they look at you, what do they see? When they think of you, do you see a smile on their faces—are they feeling loved and thankful for knowing you?

Press the pause button: *What is your dream?*

Back in November 2005 I crossed Sweden from the east to the west by myself in a kayak. I had been preparing for this expedition for several years, but I did not tell anybody of my plans until seven months before the departure. From that point on I told everybody and followed a method my team and I were working on, now called Bergersens Asymmetrical Method. This method is divided into eight steps and starts out with identifying your dream. If you follow each step, you'll end up with your dream becoming a reality. The main reason for my kayak expedition was to prove to myself that it was possible to create a method that everyone could follow that would lead to success.

As you have probably recognized, life is full of obstacles. It's as if a hidden power is trying to keep you in place. My expedition was like that as well. People around me tried to talk me out of it. There were all kinds of reasons for not doing it, for just staying at home. If I had not been following a plan, I would have never ended up in Gothenburg 16 days after I started out in Stockholm on a rainy Saturday. In the middle of the city, people were shaking their heads, smiling, as the guy with the Norwegian flag on the kayak made his way through the busy streets where families were shopping.

"What are you up to?" a guy asked. "I'm going to cross Sweden in my kayak!" I replied. "At this time of the year?" nodding his head. "Yes, and I'm starting out in an hour," I continued. Three minutes later, my trolley broke down. It was almost pitch dark when I finally began my journey next to the

Royal Swedish Castle. Two hours later, the waves grew big, and a storm hit me in the face.

"If you are not working on your dream—what are you working on?"

The words above were written down in my notebook, in the tent on an island, in the middle of Sweden in 2005. I was exhausted, cold, and insecure about the road ahead. The only reason I'm capable of telling you all this is because I had a dream, I focused on that dream, and I made all the necessary steps to make the dream become a reality. Success is the reward you'll receive when you are willing to follow your dream no matter what people around you are saying. Success is a result of failing fast and a lot and not giving up.

You are a success—it's up to you to become successful. Just remember: You are valuable whether you succeed or not! Anyway, you can ask anyone who has had success if their journey has been easy. I'm certain they all will tell you almost the same story: I have had more failures than anybody I know of, but I had a dream and a desire to reach my goal. I have been on the edge of giving up a thousand times, but I was fortunate to push through and did not give up.

"I do believe as much in the Big Bang as I believe that my children's rooms become nice and tidy just because someone throws a bomb into it."

Your key to success is you. You have all it takes to become successful and make a difference in this world. You are the only you in history. The world is waiting for your voice, your talent, your product and services. The only thing you have to do right now is put all your strength, heart, soul, and spirit into writing down your dream on a piece of paper. When you have done that, you have done something that 99.99% of the people in this world would never do. Do it. Write down your dream. Do it now!

In my book *I'm Valuable*, I wrote:

"The moment is a little gizmo sandwiched between past and future but is still all there is."

Right now, this very minute, when you read this, I'm living my dream. My son asked me the following question the other day: Dad, are you living your dream? My answer was, yes, Elias—I'm living my dream. I have written my obituary, and it's right here on my desk. I do read it from time to time to be sure I'm on track and still agree to what I have written. You are in it, my son, and so are a lot of people. It's important that we have a direction, Elias. Enjoy and be thankful for what you have right now, the gizmo sandwiched between the past and the future, and remember this:

"Impossible with a tweak is I'm possible, and so are you, my friend!"

I'm possible = YOU. Find your dream, stick to it, and include people on your journey. Repeat after me: *I'm valuable—the only me in history—and I'm bringing value to the millions of people out there who are longing to hear my voice, saying, I'm glad you stepped forward and enriched my life.*

Biography

Arthur Taubo

ARTHUR TAUBO is a professional life and business coach, speaker, artist, copywriter, graphic designer, inventor, entrepreneur, and marketeer. He has helped a lot of successful companies with their marketing and is the CEO of the company Bergersen AS—empowering greatness in people and business. He lives in Norway, is married, and has three children.

Contact Information

+47 22 07 06 20
www.twitterarthur.com
www.fbarthur.com
www.arthurtaubo.com

Chapter 13

Success Is Achieving an Unnatural Control of a Natural Process

By Doug Simpson

We succeed and fail hundreds of times every day! We do it from birth. It starts with taking that first breath of air out of the womb. We can't survive without it. It is as natural as life itself.

I have had hundreds if not thousands of successes in my lifetime. Yet I always have success goals to push toward. Success is a never-ending process. I do not believe it is a point that a person reaches but rather levels that catapult to another level of success.

Successes often, if not nearly always, are preceded by failures.

I have always been interested in business. My first business venture was as a 10-year-old, when I converted part of our backyard into a five-hole miniature golf course with the intent of charging the neighborhood kids a fee to play on it. The business failed. Maintenance, marketing, and customer demand were disasters.

I was the third child in a family of five supported by a very modest income. A job was a requirement to generate any real spending money. At the age of 11 I was selling donuts door to door after school for a local bakery. I had a cardboard box with a cloth strap around the back of my neck. To end the day back at the bakery with an empty box and money in my pocket was a success.

At 12 years of age I was unloading trucks and stocking shelves in a grocery store. I became manager of my first retail store at the age of 20. Twelve years later I was managing a 60,000-square-foot Wal-Mart store.

For that 20-year period between ages 12 and 32, I measured success with a book titled *Beat Yesterday*. Everything was measured in sales and profits today compared to yesterday and the same period last year. Success and failure were on the pages of that book. And that daily journal was validated or destroyed by the bottom line net profit percentage at the end of every year.

It was my third year as a Wal-Mart manager, and nearly halfway through my expected lifespan, I began to understand something about that book. I realized it was a record of my personal successes, but it was not the success I was really pursuing.

My life to that point was invested in the corporation. A common statement personified the corporate philosophy: "If you can't get the job done, I'll find someone who will." Disaster was always hanging a short distance in front of my face.

I realized that if anyone was going to take a serious interest in my success, it would have to me. I needed to invest in myself and my family. I made the decision to pursue a more personal quest and turned in my resignation to Wal-Mart.

Soon after, I received a personal call from Sam Walton, the founder of Wal-Mart. He said, "Doug, what are you doing? I am very happy with the way you are running your store, and the numbers are great. Why would you want to leave?"

After some discussion, I was swayed by my awe of a great entrepreneur to stay with the company. Exactly one week later, on a Friday, I was informed that I was scheduled to be in a new location in another state on the following Monday.

Here is the first key that I have to offer you. You have to decide to be successful.

That Friday was the day that my life drastically changed. I decided that day that no matter what the future held, it was of primary importance to invest in myself and my family. I could no longer leave my success in the hands of someone else, including Sam Walton. It was just too important not to take control.

My goal in life up to this point had been to hold a major position in a large corporation. But I discovered that the corporations I wanted to conquer were someone else's success, and I was only a tool to their advancing that success. I realized that even if I achieved my goal, I was just a bigger hammer in the toolbox.

Key number two is where many people falter. You have to take action on your decision.

Over the next few years after stepping toward change, I struggled with how to convert that to real results. I had made the decision and set my goal, but I did not know how to achieve it. I was guilty of depending on doing what I knew and what I thought I had succeeded at before—managing someone else's assets to make them money.

Making a decision to do something is of absolute importance. It may be a huge step to take, but no matter how big that step is, it is only a step. That decision to succeed will not create success. It will only put you in a position to take action.

After managing businesses for several companies in the city and knowing I was spinning my wheels, I made a drastic decision. I was determined to change my destiny; I went to work for a friend of mine as a carpenter's helper. That means toting wood, shoveling gravel, digging holes, and whatever else the experts needed done. I needed time to figure things out. But it didn't work. I was fired by the crew foreman for taking an unauthorized break from moving two truckloads of gravel down a hill with a wheelbarrow.

We succeed and fail many times every day. It is a natural part of us. Some successes and failures are more significant than others.

The construction contractor friend of mine who owned the company told me he had to stand behind his foreman's decision, and I fully understood that. But he had a customer who needed a sign done, and he asked me if I could make a sign. "Sure!" I said, "I've learned some construction skills."

While I was coming off the ladder after making the final touches on a hand-routed wooden sign, a man walked up to me and asked me if I had made the sign. My first personally owned business was born that day when I sold him an entrance sign for a local yacht club.

Here is the third key. Taking action requires education.

Maybe I am a slow learner. I finished college at the age of fifty. College taught me several things. If I want to learn something, I have to go get it. No one is going to drop it in my lap. If I want to succeed at something, I have to know what I am doing, but I can learn anything. I also determined that a college degree is fairly useless for much of anything but those facts.

In 1995 I discovered the Internet. At this time the World Wide Web had only recently come into existence. With a dial-up connection and some very poor instruction from the new Internet provider, I managed to download a copy of Netscape and discover a whole host of primitive websites.

It was exciting! In fact, it was so fascinating that I became possessed by it. I went from having absolutely no knowledge of computers or the Internet to being the IT and online manager for a network of newspapers.

Education comes through immersing yourself in your desired field. Education requires experience, study, determination, and commitment. You cannot get it in college.

I learned a lot about building an online business, advertising, marketing, image building, and more while working for the newspaper.

The experience confirmed an observation that I had made several times throughout my business life. It reaffirmed in my mind that there are not many experts out there. And many of the few who are experts have no idea of the value of their expertise.

That brings me to the fourth key—analyze daily.

Success without daily analysis progresses at a very slow pace if at all.

In retail, business analysis is vital to survival. You must analyze every product you stock: its sales rate, profit margin, inventory requirements, turnover, retail price, and many other factors. Things like payroll, advertising, and all the things that affect your overhead costs are crucial to profits. Your store location, the color and layout of your sign, your customer entrance and exit, the store layout, and hundreds of other factors affect success or failure.

My first real attempt at my own business never opened its doors to the public. During the setup stage, analysis of what I thought was a great plan showed it would fail. I successfully started and sold my next two businesses. Analysis showed me that although they could survive, neither business would achieve the goals I had set for myself. For me to succeed, they would have to go so I could move on.

One of my current businesses is a retail store, mainly doing business online. It now ships out hundreds of orders comprising dozens of carefully chosen products every month. One of the advantages of online businesses is the large amount of analytical information available. This information allows for daily tweaking of a business. Analysis and adjustment are critical to advancing sales and profitability.

I had finally arrived at the point where I could concentrate full time on developing my own success. This is a place that most of the great leaders of the world discovered much earlier than I did.

Key number five—help someone else achieve success.

I believe one of the biggest keys to building a business is to provide a service for someone else. I am not talking about devising a service and selling it. I am talking about filling other people's needs.

There is an old saying in sales about the man who buys a drill. He doesn't really want a drill; he wants a well-placed hole. The expert precision of a quality power drill in the hands of the man produces a perfect hole.

This key birthed my latest business. I believe many people have a power drill in their tool box. Some don't know how to use it. And others don't know where to place the hole. My success today is watching the excitement in people who realize they have expert equipment and begin to use their power to make holes where they want them.

Key number six is critical—repeat the first five!

Success takes application of the first five principles in combination perpetually repeated. In my opinion, this is where 95% of people fail. It is the most difficult step of all. It might even be summed up in a single word—focus.

As I said in the beginning, we succeed and fail hundreds of times a day! We constantly make decisions, take action, learn from the results, analyze, and repeat. It is our nature as humans. We do it from birth.

So if that is the case, why aren't we all huge successes? We fail because it becomes automatic instead of intentional. Unless we direct this process in our lives, we will simply take the path of least resistance.

Imagine a mountain river that flows through the valleys, following the path of least resistance. Rain and melting snow send beautiful fresh water cascading down the landscape. It supports fish, wildlife, people, crops, and who knows what else. But if the rain and snow stop, the river dries up, and everything dependent on it suffers.

What if man creates a resistance that the river cannot overcome? He builds a dam. He now controls the resources of the river, maintains all its previous benefits, and prevents it from drying up downstream. But not only that, he also creates whole new industries of recreation, fish and wildlife management, marina sales and services, guide services, boat and yacht sales and repair, and more. Now not only is he able to sell the water, but he is able to put it to work creating electricity that affects an unlimited number of areas. All of these create jobs and revenue that did not previously exist.

He has focused the available resources and manages them with decisions, actions, education, and analysis. And in the process he has helped thousands of people.

Success is controlling the minute-by-minute flow of our lives by focusing our internal and external resources. We control that by constructing a focal point much like a dam. We let nothing pass that we have not taken control of. This is what I call unnatural control of a natural process.

Are you ready to do something unnatural?

Biography

Doug Simpson

DOUG SIMPSON is owner and CEO of Artplace, Inc.
He has 35 years' experience in retail management and
business development and ownership and holds a BA
degree in art education. Doug spent 15 years as an IT and
online manager for a newspaper network and has been
operating online businesses for more than 15 years. Using
his retail, marketing, advertising, Internet, and public relations experience,
he currently assists people in elevating their unique experiences to an expert
level in their market.

Contact Information

Artplace, Inc.
413 W. Main St.
Denison, TX 75020
888-219-4561
doug@doug-simpson.com
www.artplace.com
www.doug-simpson.com

Chapter 14

The Secret Ingredient to Success

By Kathryn Thomas

$\mathcal{D}$o you feel like you've been going through all the "right" motions and still the success you desire eludes you? Do you think that, somewhere in your studies, you must have missed something important? Perhaps you're correct!

For many years, I chased after the money. I felt that personal and professional success would come once the money started flowing. So as I built my business, I would also be guaranteeing my success, and all my dreams would come true. But it didn't work out that way at all. In fact, I did all the "right" things in several different careers before I left them all behind and just went after what I was passionate about.

I could have saved years of time and frustration if I had only realized that *success comes from the mind—not from the money*. Although I had a true desire to succeed, what I kept trying to succeed at was unfulfilling. I sabotaged my own success (several times) because what I really wanted deep within me was success in something else. Once I figured that out and started doing something I have a natural talent and passion for, things finally started falling into place.

Passion in Action

Whatever type of success you seek, your success always begins within you. Whether you're seeking wealth, good health, a loving relationship, or a more fulfilling life, going through all the "right" motions may move you forward, but it rarely gets you to your ultimate goal without true passion.

Passion will always enable you to find a way to get what you want,
regardless of the challenges that rise up to try to stop you.

John Belushi said it well in the classic movie *The Blues Brothers*: "We're on a mission from God." Even though *The Blues Brothers* movie has a purpose other than motivation or inspiration, just think of all the challenges Jake and Elwood Blues faced in getting the money to the tax collector's office to save the nuns. Yet because they felt that they were on a divine mission, they were filled with passion for their goal, and nothing could stop them!

You can see passion in action in all successful movies. Passion always motivates the hero to defy the odds to overcome all challenges.

Leaving the movies for real life, think about every successful person you know. Regardless of what they're a success at—their career, sports, a hobby, their marriage, telling jokes, or juggling—do you think they would have achieved what they did if they didn't really care about reaching their goal?

Someone I looked up to my entire adult life—my high school English teacher—recently completed his journey on this earth, leaving a legacy of success in the students he devoted his life to. His passing extinguished the flame of one of the most passionate, successful people I'll ever have the pleasure of meeting. But he shines on brightly in the many people who attribute their success to him—from doctors and scientists to housewives who devote their lives to caring for their family.

Was he wealthy? No.

Was he famous? No.

Was he a celebrity? No.

But he enjoyed success. Do you think he cared? Of course he did. He cared with a passion that cannot be matched and lived a joyful, fulfilling life. RIP J.K.

With passion, you, too, can enjoy many pinnacles of success in your life!

In fact, you've most likely used your passion to achieve many successes without even realizing it.

The Fuel for Your Fire

Remember when you were a kid learning to ride a bike? How much did you want it? Were you determined to master it regardless of how many times you fell? Do you even remember how many times you fell?

As you soon discovered, falling was only part of the inevitable process, not the end result. So you kept your eye on your goal. Each time you fell, you learned to try it a little differently. You got back up and tried again and again until you achieved success. Today, you don't remember how many times you fell—only that you learned to ride a bike!

A familiar saying that you've most likely heard is, "Oh, this is like riding a bike. Once you learn it, you never forget." In reflection, you can see how that statement applies to *any* success. *Once you figure out the secret to getting what you want, success is just like riding a bike.*

That secret is your passion. It's passion that lights a fire inside you and keeps you going until you reach your goal. It encourages you to seek solutions to your challenges so you can continue moving forward. It prevents you from giving up when the going gets tough. And *it gives you the power to make your dreams come true.*

Discovering Your Passions

To discover the passions that have the power to fuel your success, look within. Determine what makes you tick. What do you enjoy the most? Answering these questions will help you figure out what you're most passionate about:

- If you could do anything you wanted, and money was no object, what would you choose to do? Why?
- Where would you like to live? Visit? Why?
- Whom would you like to go with? Why?
- What do you enjoy doing during your leisure time? Do you pursue hobbies? What are they?
- Do you find strength, joy, or inspiration in your religious beliefs?

- Are you strongly committed to a political ideology?
- What are you good at? This will enlighten you to some of your natural talents.
- Does helping others bring you joy?
- Are pets or wild animals involved in your life?
- Do you enjoy being around children?
- What times in your life were your happiest? Why? What passions filled these moments?
- What dreams would you like to bring to life?

These questions might lead you to further ideas not mentioned here that are important to you as well. Write them all down. In reflecting on your answers, you'll be able to clarify your passions. Plus, you may find out things about yourself that you never even realized were so critical to what you really want!

Turning Your Passions into a Powerful Force for Success

Now that you know what you're most passionate about, how can you use this information to make your dreams come true?

Follow these action tips to allow your passions to guide you to a life filled with success:

1. **Visualize the details.** It's important to picture yourself living in fulfillment of your dreams. Put yourself in your happy place. Imagine every single detail—as if you're there in body as well as mind. Create the scene as if you've already achieved your goal.

   - *Note your perceptions coming in from every sense.* What do you see, hear, feel, smell, and taste?
   - *Feel your emotions.* Joy, happiness, pride in your achievement, gratitude, excitement, contentment, and satisfaction may all be represented. Stay with your visualization for a few minutes to give

yourself time to totally enjoy these feelings. Suspend reality and immerse yourself in this moment of intense positive feelings. Feel free to laugh, cry tears of gratitude and joy, and otherwise express your emotions.

- *An intense, positive mental and physical experience like this helps bring out your passions.* In addition, it triggers psychological activities in your mind that naturally guide you there in real life. You'll find it easier to make decisions and take actions that lead you to achieve your goals.

2. **Purposefully create the life you desire.** Your passion will make the difference between living a life of tedium and one abundant with the excitement of success. When you live your life "on purpose," you literally choose what you do with your life each day. Use these strategies to help you make choices that are in alignment with your passions:

- *Ask yourself, "Does this work for me?"* If you feel like something in your life isn't working for you, then it's really working against you. Determine what *will* work for you instead and make the decision to change your circumstances. Then take action to make the change happen. If it's a big change, divide your task into small, achievable steps and then follow your plan.

- *Use positive self-talk to inspire and encourage.* Imagine what it would be like if someone were right beside you all day, every day to encourage you along. Wouldn't you try harder? Wouldn't you be more inspired to make positive decisions? The good news is you *do* have such a person! You talk to yourself all day long and *you can control what you say!* Get into the habit of saying things to yourself that you *want* to hear. Each time you have a negative thought, immediately change it to a positive one. Be your own cheerleader and help yourself create the life you desire with positive self-talk.

- *Believe in yourself. Know that you deserve success.* You were created totally unique, with a set of passions and talents unlike anyone else's. Honor the magnificent creation you are by recognizing your passions and developing your natural talents. As a result, you'll live in harmony with your inner self and find that the life you deserve is one of success and fulfillment.

3. **Enjoy the journey.** While your passions move you forward toward a better life, they also help you enjoy where you are right now. When you allow this to happen by seeing what's good in your life, it moves you closer to where you want to be.

    • Motivational author and speaker Dr. Joe Vitale has often said that *the fastest way to get to where you want to be is to be happy where you are.* There are several reasons why this works. When you're happy with your life, your mind resonates in harmony with happiness and brings more happiness to you. When you have gratitude, that feeling attracts more things for you to be thankful for. So enjoying the life you have helps you create the life you want.

    • *Live in the moment.* Life is a parade of moments. If you try to put off living while focusing on your goals, one day you may wake up to find that your parade has passed you by! Don't let this happen to you! Take time to stop and smell the roses. Find something to cherish about each moment. Let your passions guide you to get what you want out of each experience.

Is living in alignment with your passions the secret ingredient that has been missing in your life? When you set your goals and make action plans according to what's most important to you, you're more likely to achieve them. Passion motivates you to overcome challenges and moves you to make positive choices that help bring your goals to fruition.

With passion, you can leave complacency behind and move joyfully into success!

Biography

Kathryn Thomas

As a successful life coach and writer, KATHRYN THOMAS enjoys using her training, education, and experience to help others reach important goals in their lives. *"Yes, You CAN Create the Life You Desire"* is her motto. You can find inspiring tips, techniques, and strategies for bringing your dreams to life at her blog: KathrynLThomas.com. Feel free  to send in your questions, comments, and opinions by submitting the "Contact Me" form.

Contact Information

KathrynLThomas.com

Chapter 15

The Entrepreneurial Rebound

HOW TO SURVIVE AND THRIVE
AFTER EXPERIENCING FAILURE

By William D. Baker

As we drove away I could see her in my rearview mirror, sitting on the doorstep of our old home and sobbing uncontrollably. We were moving away and leaving her behind. Shannon, who was 17 at the time, had grown up in our home as the best friend of the eldest of my three daughters, and now, just like that, we were traveling 3,000 miles away. As we turned out of the driveway, all my daughters joined the frenzy with sobbing tears and gut-wrenching sounds, as if pieces of their hearts had been torn from their bodies. It was the toughest thing I had ever done, but I was compelled by a force so strong that it pushed me forward on a huge tidal wave of hope and anticipation. It hurt to leave, but I knew that in the long run it would be better for all of us. My life's journey had taken a decidedly different direction—West. I was leaving to start again after the bitter, disappointing failure of a business I had spent years developing and that was at one time a rising star in its industry.

Virtually every successful entrepreneur has failed and then recovered. Some of them several times. From Thomas Edison to Donald Trump, they have all experienced failure. What about you? Have you ever been challenged to pick yourself up from a stunning defeat and start again? The ability to bounce back from unsuccessful attempts at building an enterprise is one of the most valuable traits an entrepreneur can possess while working toward ultimate, lasting success. From front line experience, however, I can say that when you are going through it, all you want is for everything to be better again.

Failure (sometimes called "learning experiences") puts a huge strain on personal and professional relationships. No one wants to be around someone who has just flopped big time, but it does filter out true friends. Frankly, it's not much fun, and because of that, most people fear failure and avoid it by simply not trying to be successful in the first place. To me, not trying is the biggest failure of all, and not trying again (i.e., rebounding) wastes all the effort and experience of the previous failures.

My own rebound opportunity came just after my 31st birthday.

When I was 21, I set a goal to become a millionaire before I turned 30. I was a year late. In my 31st year I owned 1 million shares of a company that was trading at $3, and on paper I had a net worth of $3 million. I was flying high and living the good life until it all came crashing down a year later.

I grew up the second of seven children in a family that didn't have much money. My dad was an enlisted soldier with all of us to feed, and my mom was a full-time homemaker. We got by, but baloney and peanut butter were staples. I longed for something more, something better, something that would propel me to financial wealth and independence. That dream burned deeply and motivated me to get a university education and learn about business.

I received some help from the Canadian military, which granted me a full scholarship in exchange for a four-year tour of duty. I soon discovered that the military was not a place for an independent-thinking entrepreneur who wanted to control his own destiny. I left to pursue my dream of owning a business. I surmised that the best way to learn business was from observing other businesses, and I chose to become a chartered accountant to quickly gain an insider's view of successful companies. This turned out to be an excellent decision as I learned a great deal about how a variety of businesses worked.

I learned about business models, cash flow, and even some marketing, but I knew that working as an accountant was not really my passion. I needed to get into a business of my own. I had taken a job with a venture capital company in Ottawa and a few years later found an opportunity that captivated me. It was with a fledgling telecommunications company that had a terrific new product.

After a small initial investment, the VC company became distracted with other investments, so I convinced them to sell me their shares and became president of the small company, working with the much older founder, who was a sales and promotions specialist. Together we drove the company right into the ground. We raised millions of dollars, took the company public, and built a full manufacturing facility. The product was a marvel of engineering and technological advances at the time. It was a full telephone in desk blotter format and contained various advanced features that appealed to executives. It was a stunner . . . on paper.

Sales of the product were made before it could be delivered bug free, and the challenge of getting engineering fixes into manufacturing quickly proved overwhelming. It was like trying to build an airplane while it was already in the air. Ultimately the company failed, and along with it, my total net worth disappeared. I also had to tell 200 people that their jobs were gone. I had borrowed heavily to finance the purchase of stock in the company, and the bank called my loan. I had no way to pay. I was broke and had a growing family to support. It was a desperate time, and I was forced into survival mode, including using the bankruptcy act to settle with my creditors. It was only many years later that the learning and character-building aspects of this difficult experience became apparent.

Using my skills in financing corporations, I began doing some consulting work and then came across another opportunity to build a world-class company. I once again dived into entrepreneurial waters and began paddling furiously. This time would be different, I thought. The company became a leader in the newly emerging in-store media business and was on its way to becoming a successful public company when disaster struck. We were just in the process of marketing the initial public offering when the U.S. invaded Iraq and all hell broke loose. The markets crashed and IPOs were shelved. Our offering was canceled and never resurrected. Eventually, without the capital needed to expand, the company disappeared. Strike two. Back to start.

I once heard Charles "Tremendous" Jones, the legendary motivational speaker, say something that simplified life's choices. He said there were only three things you needed to decide in life: where to live, who to live with, and what to do with your life. Fortunately I had married a very supportive woman who provided a stable foundation for my entrepreneurial ventures. I now wanted to nail down the first of these—where to live. I had grown increasingly unhappy with Ottawa's harsh winters and hot, humid summers. I longed for somewhere I could spend more time outdoors. That place was British Columbia. I had visited the previous year, and not only was the climate better, but the energy was different—vibrant, alive, and full of unlimited possibilities. I decided to move there at the earliest possible opportunity. That opportunity came shortly after my second company failed, when I needed once again to stage a rebound.

My wife, Elizabeth, and I sold the house, said our goodbyes, and off we went. My little band of sobbing sisters, my wife, and I drove away in our overstuffed van, leaving behind friends, family, and numerous business and social contacts that we had built up over 20 years. Off to a new beginning, a new horizon, and a new home in North Vancouver, where there were mountains, oceans, and an upbeat energy, with the highest per capita number of work-at-home entrepreneurs in the country. With little money, no job, no contacts, and no plan of where to begin, we rented a house, and I began a campaign of rebuilding. Ultimately, I ended up with a company that now provides financial empowerment to growing companies, including managing a multimillion-dollar venture capital fund to assist companies in the early stages of development. I love working with visionary entrepreneurs.

A year after moving to B.C., my wife and daughters not only forgave me for yanking them out of their comfortable world in Ottawa but actually thanked me. They came to love the West and all its exciting possibilities. The vision of the sobbing girl sitting on a doorstep in Ottawa still haunts me, but since that time, she has made multiple trips out to visit us.

The move to B.C. energized me, provided me with unique opportunities, and allowed me to regain the confidence I needed to pick up and try again. As a result, I have finally made it. A wonderful family, a nice home with a fabulous view of the mountains and ocean, lots of money in the bank, a growing investment portfolio, and the excitement and satisfaction of helping other people realize their dreams while fulfilling my own. I consider my journey still very much in progress, but let me pause for a moment to pass on my baker's dozen of lessons I've learned in the art of successful rebounding:

1. **The meek shall not inherit the earth**; rather, the strong and articulate shall rule, so join Toastmasters and be bold.

2. **If it isn't working, move out of your groove** and carve a new one.

3. **Fear is good** but needs to be harnessed. Overcome the fear of failure by pitting it against the fear of living an irrelevant life.

4. **If you can dream it, you can make it happen.** If you have the capacity to dream and clearly visualize what you desire most, you can fulfill that dream. But if you don't take continual action to move forward, then you won't ever get to that wonderful place of achieving your dreams. The world belongs to dreamers, but only those who can overcome their fear and take action. The law of action beats the law of attraction.

5. **Goals are the indispensable partners of dreams.** Setting goals and creating a detailed plan to achieve them are the way to enjoy a sumptuous feast at the banquet of life.

6. **When you fail, don't panic.** Remain calm and strategize a way out of the predicament. There is always a way up, over, or around a temporary setback. Have alternatives so that if one thing doesn't work, you can move on to another. **Action subdues panic.**

7. **Have an emergency exit.** Whenever you move into a new (or existing) enterprise, set up your emergency exit. Put aside money and resources that can be accessed if things go horribly wrong. The recovery fund should be well out of the reach of potential creditors. It is infinitely easier to rebound if you aren't worried about how you are going to feed your family.

8. **Explosive anger at a person, situation, or bureaucracy (especially tax departments) rarely helps solve a problem.** Focus on the desired outcome and work on making it happen. Then, go out into the woods and scream as loud as you can and release all the pent-up anger and frustration. The trees don't mind.

9. **If you're knocked down, get back up** and make a point to avoid that particular punch the next time. The only time you are beat is if you don't get back up and try again. Also . . . buy the best boxing gloves you can afford.

10. **Find a worthwhile charity, service club, or volunteer opportunity and get involved.** This not only brings some balance to your life but will return far more to you in spiritual and material benefits than you give. When I moved to B.C. I joined the Kiwanis Club and received numerous benefits from the organization even though that wasn't why I became involved.

11. **Be inspired by winners but take a close look at them**—most have rebounded from a defeat themselves, so also be inspired by the adversity they have overcome.

12. **Incorporate continual learning as part of your life**—invest in yourself by taking courses, attending seminars, reading relevant books and magazines, and listening to CDs. You will routinely be inspired by an idea or way of thinking that could make a huge difference in your life. Both your mind and your dreams will expand.

13. **Seek a mentor or small mastermind group** of business people to share ideas with—it's amazing how your thinking will be altered through discussions with trusted advisers.

I have been fortunate to have had a lot of success in my life, and in truth, that success means much more because of the painful failures that came before it. I'm not recommending you go out and seek failure as a learning experience, but if you are out there pushing your own envelope and trying to make things happen to accomplish goals and dreams, eventually you will fail. How you handle your failure and subsequent rebound is what will make the difference between fulfilling your dreams and filing your dreams. Failure is a by-product of entrepreneurialism and needs to be incorporated in the process of success. The ability to stage a rebound is a valuable tool in the entrepreneur's toolkit and gives you an instant affinity with all the other failed but now successful entrepreneurs. Like all of life's most important lessons, however, it must be experienced. I hope your rebound is swift and much less difficult than mine. Remember, success is waiting just a rebound away. Never give up.

Biography

William D. Baker

WILLIAM D. BAKER, CA, is a serial entrepreneur who has over the past 40 years started numerous companies in various industries, including telecommunications, Internet, publishing, financial services, and media. Some of these were spectacular failures, and a few were wonderfully successful. He is the author of *Commando*  *Financing . . . How to Realize Your Dreams Using Other People's Money.* He currently manages an investment fund specializing in fast-growing early stage companies and mentors their entrepreneurs. Bill and his wife live in British Columbia, Canada.

Contact Information

Willabeth Capital Corporation
200-100 Park Royal S.
West Vancouver, BC, Canada V7T1A2
604-980-7265
bbaker@willabeth.com
www.willabeth.com

Chapter 16
The Landfill of Your Mind

By Midori Dunn

Have you ever gone to a city dump? You get there, pay, pull up to the dumping area, and then proceed to dump all of your trash and garbage into the landfill. Many times, you are not the only one there dumping. Just like the landfill of your mind. Whether you realize it or not, you have been dumped on throughout the years. Some of it garbage, some of it treasure. Subliminal messages are everywhere. No matter where we turn, there is some sort of message invading our mental environment, be it from family, friends, school, work, daily conversations, TV, or social media. We are constantly exposed to a multitude of thoughts and ideas. Before we know it, these thoughts become deeply ingrained in us, and they penetrate our belief systems and show up in our results.

I became keenly aware of this one day when I allowed myself to be overwhelmed with emotions. I realized that my underlying belief system was undermining my ability to achieve the level of success I desired. I was astonished at how much mental garbage I had let accumulate in my personal landfill. It was self-sabotage in action.

"You're living a lie you know."

"No, I'm not."

"Yes, you are, my delusional friend. You lie to yourself on a daily basis. The sad part is, you just accept it as fact. You head down the road of destruction every time you doubt your ability and question your self-worth."

"Why are you saying those things? What do you know? You're just a voice I hear in my head."

"I know more than you know."

"For argument's sake, let's say you're right. What can I do to change? I really am tired of letting myself down all the time. I feel sick to my stomach when I do so. I have great ideas, and I talk a good game, but when it comes down to it, I end up talking myself out of things before I ever get started. I let the voices in my head conjure up fear and self-doubt, and it paralyzes me. What can I do?"

"You just have to remember."

"Remember what?"

"The truth."

"The truth. What truth?"

"You were born to succeed. It is your birthright. Think back to when you were a baby. Success was second nature to you. You never questioned or doubted your ability. You just made forward progress. I'm sure that when you learned to walk for the first time, you fell many times on your diapered derriere. I guarantee you didn't sit there and think to yourself, It's not worth the effort. I'll just keep crawling instead. Heck no! You grabbed a hold of the table or couch, pulled yourself up, took a step, and promptly fell again. You did this over and over again until you achieved your goal of walking for the first time. You were amazing to watch."

"Really?"

"Yes, really. Your persistence, determination, focus, excitement, and belief in yourself were key attributes to your success. You didn't let anything derail you from your desired end result. You kept on moving forward no matter what. You innately knew that success was yours and that you were definitely worth the effort."

Grateful for the honesty of this internal dialogue, I wiped away the tears streaming down my face. I looked intensely into the eyes of my reflection and said, "I apologize for letting you down all these years. You have the seeds of success already planted in you. I love you and I believe in you. I will make you proud. I promise."

"I already am."

This internal conversation was such a blessing for me. It woke me up to the fact that I was setting myself up to fail over and over again. I was carrying around so much garbage in my mental landfill. Fear, doubt, and regret dominated. I let my thoughts get the best of me, and they took me in a downward spiral. I was emotionally drained and mentally worn out. Something had to change. My thoughts turned out to be the prime candidate.

Self-Created Roadblocks

What did I have to do to get past these self-created roadblocks? I had to take control of my thoughts and take full responsibility for the results I generated. First of all, I had to let go of those thoughts that did not serve me. I had to release the feelings of sadness and the pain of regret that came from losing five close family members, including my mom, in an 11-month time frame. I had to forgive myself for letting my insecurities, lack of self-confidence, and low self-esteem cause me to make decisions that ultimately ended in my husband and me losing our house, having to close down our franchise business, and losing hundreds of thousands of dollars in the process.

Going through these events, one right after the other, was quite devastating. I thought about curling up in bed, pulling the covers over my head, and wallowing in my self-pity. Instead of succumbing to that temptation, I decided to look at these life experiences with an attitude of appreciation and to see them as blessings. It's been very liberating to acknowledge the error in my ways and to admit to the mistakes I've made. Life lessons can sometimes be extremely costly, but they are always valuable.

A Matter of Choice

Chasing after your dreams takes guts and gumption. It may not always turn out as planned, but it is definitely worth the effort. Some people may say that my husband and me failed because we lost so-called everything. Failure is on the path to success. It is not on the opposite end. I believe we succeeded because we failed. We took a risk and went after our dream. We worked hard, endured many setbacks, and experienced great loss. Does that mean we give up on our dream of having the time freedom and financial resources to be able to choose how we spend our daily moments? Of course not.

"Choice, not circumstances, determines your success."
—Anonymous

Everything in life is a choice, from the moment we wake up until the moment we lay our head down to sleep. In fact, we choose how we wake up in the morning—whether it be to an alarm clock, our children, the sound of waves rolling on the shore—or just rolling over and going back to sleep. The choice is ours, plain and simple.

Achieving success is just the same. It is a matter of choice. You choose to be a winner, a champion, a hero, or otherwise. Thoughts have amazing creative power. They have the ability to build you up or knock you down. It is actually the choice you make that determines the road you take. Therefore, do everything in your power to protect and empower your mental, physical, emotional, and spiritual environment. Truly successful people do that. They take control of their overall well-being. They engage in activities that move them toward their ideal life and are congruent with their values and priorities. W. Clement Stone said, "You are a product of your environment. So choose the environment that will best develop you toward your objective. Analyze your life in terms of its environment. Are the things around you helping you toward success—or are they holding you back?"

Although success is usually referred to with a positive connotation, I believe that we are a success at everything we do whether it has a positive outcome or a negative one. Once our tendencies are developed, we are successful in achieving similar results every time we act accordingly. It is said that how you do anything is how you do everything. Therefore, be conscious and aware of your mental chatter and your daily habits. They are a perfect gauge to determine whether you are being your own worst enemy or your own best friend. It always baffles me to see how our tendency usually takes us toward the critical side. Of all the people we come in contact with, the one we should be a best friend to is the person we live with day in and day out . . . ourselves.

The lesson learned is that it all comes down to the choices you make. The success you experience or the lack thereof is the result of the choices you've made throughout your lifetime. Wow! That can be a huge pill to swallow. It means taking full responsibility for where you are in life. If you are pleased with your current results . . . fantastic. If you are not, guess what? You can make different choices, thus creating different results.

Success Is in the Eye of the Beholder

It is very important to define what success means to you. Many times we are just going through the motions, assuming that we are on the right track to success. However, most of us never take the time to really dig deep to discover what really drives us. This must be done before we can ever move forward effectively in its direction. Take some well-deserved quiet time and consume yourself with defining success through your eyes and your eyes only. After all, success is in the eye of the beholder.

Figure out what you choose your life to be about. What do you stand for? If you are up for a fun exercise, then I recommend that you write out your eulogy. It may sound a bit strange and somewhat morbid, but it gets you focused, purposeful, intentional, and it reveals your life's vision. Be as imaginative, creative, and detailed as possible. Once you are clear and you can feel the passion rise up from inside you, then declare it with boldness, confidence, and belief that it is done. Remember, you are creating a life designed to your specifications.

Promise Yourself

Several years ago, I came across this quote from Christian D. Larson. It has served me well over the years and has kept my perspective on life in check. It is definitely a great philosophy and one that I choose to live by.

Promise Yourself
- To be strong that nothing can disturb your peace of mind.
- To talk health, happiness, and prosperity to every person you meet.
- To make all your friends feel that there is something worthwhile in them.
- To look at the sunny side of everything and make your optimism come true.

- To think only of the best, to work only for the best, and to expect only the best.

- To be just as enthusiastic about the success of others as you are about your own.

- To forget the mistakes of the past and press on to the greater achievements of the future.

- To wear a cheerful expression at all times and give a smile to every living creature you meet.

- To give so much time to improving yourself that you have no time to criticize others.

- To be too large for worry, too noble for anger, too strong for fear, and too happy to permit the presence of trouble.

- To think well of yourself and to proclaim this fact to the world, not in loud words, but in great deeds.

- To live in the faith that the whole world is on your side, so long as you are true to the best that is in you.

Allow these powerful words to soak into your being. Make this a daily deposit into the landfill of your mind. Promise yourself that you are worth the effort. Enjoy being your own hero. Success is in you. Always has been, always will be.

Biography
Midori Dunn

Born and raised in Hawaii, MIDORI DUNN grew up surrounded by the spirit of love, family, and friends. From being the first girl to play on her high school varsity boys' golf team to earning a college degree to playing golf professionally on the mini tours to experiencing the ups and downs of business ownership, Midori has learned the  importance and value of empowering your overall environment and having an attitude of appreciation. She speaks and trains on the power of personal development, continuing self-education, taking personal responsibility, and sending out positive messages. Midori Dunn loves being a wife, mom, friend, entrepreneur, author, speaker, facilitator, volunteer, and gifted communicator. She utilizes her life experiences and enjoys sharing psychological insight and inspired communication with people to encourage and empower them to discover their dreams again, believe in themselves, and know they are worth the effort.

Contact Information

877-617-2996
Midori@MidoriDunn.com
www.MidoriDunn.com

Chapter 17

From Business Failure to Personal Selling Success

By Chin MC

Thirteen years ago, Mr. Ng Fook Choy failed in his shoe accessories business. Not only did the bank foreclose on the factories, he also had to sell the house he and his wife and their two-year-old son were living in. The only car, which he needed badly for his livelihood, was repossessed.

Despite selling all his assets, he was able to repay only part of his outstanding loans. Like some who have met with the same fate and come out stronger, he struggled to regain his self-worth.

He started off as a distributor of insurance-related medical cards for Integrated Health Management (IHM), a healthcare company, in 1998. He fought hard to achieve his personal sales targets. Today he holds the top position as a regional manager earning at least RM100,000 (US $33,333) a year.

In 2003, he became an agent for an insurance-related savings plan with Allianz, an insurance company. He sought help from his mentor, who was a top insurance consultant. He moved up in rank to a career agent and earned Million Dollar Round Table awards five times based on his personal sales. The last criterion he qualified for, in 2010, was a RM420,000 (US $140,000) first-year premium.

He is very humble about his success as he reflects on how devastated he was 13 years earlier. He was humiliated. Some close friends deserted him, but he picked himself up with a "do or die" attitude, and with his willingness to learn and his unshakable determination, he became who he is today.

His Background

Mr. Ng, a Malaysian in his late 40s, was brought up by his father, a government servant who passed away when he was a teenager, and his mother, who is a housewife. Growing up on the pension of his late father with an elder sister and two younger brothers was financially challenging. They all had to seek employment immediately or a few years after their schooling years.

He attended the same school I went to, and schooling was a bit of a struggle for us. But he obtained a diploma in accounting (LCCI); then he studied for a professional accounting qualification (ACCA), which I also have.

He stopped after passing two papers in 1984 to start his first job as an accounts clerk with a plywood factory. He left after six months to work as secretary to a politician.

Four years later, the politician offered him a chance to become an entrepreneur. He grabbed the offer to start the shoe accessories business in 1988, not realizing that it required great business acumen.

The business thrived for a number of years, but when China stormed the world with its cheaper alternative, his sales went down drastically, as did his competitors'. The suppliers stopped supplying, workers had to ask to be paid, and his credit cards were canceled.

When the banks started demanding loan repayment, I had full knowledge of it as I worked in one of those banks back then. He missed a big opportunity to sell the mortgaged factories because the bank was not willing to negotiate at a price just a little short of the outstanding loan.

His wife, who was looking after their two-year-old boy, was forced to go back to work with her previous employer in a garment factory. Their son was sent to a day care center while both husband and wife worked.

Success to him, then, meant earning enough to pay off the balance of the loan and still have enough to lead a more than comfortable lifestyle.

His Big Break and Challenges

In his desperate search for work, three friends recommended commission-based jobs, which he had doubts about initially. But he realized that working for a fixed salary would take him many years to earn enough to pay off the balance of the loan he still owed, and starting another business was simply out of the question, so he took on the commission-based jobs.

The first friend introduced him to a healthcare company, where he became a medical card distributor. He had to swallow his pride and knock on the doors of his contacts from his previous business.

Competition was fierce, but he survived, for he had to succeed no matter how difficult it was. Doing that also led him to improve his selling skills. Seeing at least ten customers a day was the norm. He had to sacrifice many weekends promoting medical cards at hospitals and traveling out of town to give sales talks. He loves to render after-sales service, like seeing card holders admitted to hospitals and giving advice on which doctors to consult. He quipped that he is like a doctor on call. Medical card holders have to see him first before consulting a medical doctor! Thus, even on the first day of Chinese New Year 2003, he had to attend to hospital admission.

Frequent visits to hospitals were really a blessing in disguise because he got on the radar screen of most of the doctors he would approach about a mutual fund company and the insurance-related savings plan he later ventured into.

One embarrassing incident he will never forget was when he first started, he had to wait until he received his commission checks to pay a mere RM36 (US $12) monthly newspaper fee! He is proud to be in a position to say that such a thing will not happen to him again.

Mr. Ng took on a second job as a mutual fund agent to boost his income stream. However, he soon realized that selling mutual funds was not his cup of tea. He struggled to make sales, and after a year and a half, he gave up and focused on his strength in insurance sales.

That was when he paid attention to his successful insurance agent friend, whose luxurious lifestyle motivated Mr. Ng to take on his third job as an agent. Again he approached his list of medical card customers, and a miracle happened—most of them were responsive to his sales presentation.

He was willing to train and seek counsel, so he was mentored to become a leader. He went into the training with great determination to succeed—he embraced the system—and he worked really hard. That was the secret to his success in the insurance savings plan sales.

He always looks upon the late Tan Sri Lim Goh Tong, the founder of Genting Highlands—a casino and entertainment enterprise—for his vision, energy, and drive. And his own motto is to become the best person you can be, set realistic goals, and set your heart, mind, and soul in achieving them.

His 10 core success mindset habits are:

1. Believing in himself and enjoying his work
2. Seeing his success daily through visualization and affirmation
3. Attending all product and personal development training
4. Rendering after-sales service and advice to existing customers
5. Filling his appointment book and meeting potential customers every day
6. Following up with potential customers to close sales
7. Monitoring sales and adjusting strategies to meet sales targets
8. Making new contacts at networking functions or simply getting out in the streets
9. Sharing success to motivate each other in the same industry
10. Spending meaningful time with family at home and on vacations

Looking back, Mr. Ng realized why he had failed in his earlier business. He had neither management nor leadership skills. He was not all that familiar with the business. And he missed seeing the trend that the sun was setting on that industry.

He now understands that leadership has a lot to do with continuous learning, leading by example, and working hard to achieve his goals. Right now, he sees a trend that other agents are embracing—computers and the Internet—and not to be left behind, he has engaged my service to train him to be successful in growing his business online.

Conclusion

Not deterred by his business failure, Mr. Ng decided that he had to change his life forever. He knew it was a gamble to take on commissioned jobs that he had no prior knowledge and experience doing, but he did not have any better choice. His success proved that he had indeed made the right decision.

His commission-based compensation has its advantages—he now earns recurring income, and he can certainly afford to spend more time with his wife and his son, who is now 15. He is earning a more than comfortable income as a regional manager with IHM and career agent with Allianz. His success is based solely on his personal effort, as he has not started to play the recruitment game yet. He is confident many will look up to him with trust and respect for his personal leadership when he establishes his own team to grow his sales.

What he had was great determination to get himself out of the financial rut by not letting failure break his fighting spirit. He became a leader and achieved great job satisfaction.

Biography

Chin MC

An accountant with banking experience, CHIN MC trains business owners to be successful in growing their businesses online. He has conducted credit writing courses for commercial banks; written and sold a competitive article, "How to Get Your Bank Loan Restructured"; and written a give-away eBook, *How to Start a Hosting Reseller's*  *Business*. He is a certified NLP practitioner, a qualified accountant, and holds a master's degree in training.

Contact Information

6-012-5195005
www.GettingLocalBusinessOnline.com

Chapter 18

The Power Is Yours!

By Julia J. Mueller

The beginning of the '90s presented an unexpected turn of events in my life. Let's just cut right to it. I was brutally beaten within an inch of my life, by a person whom I thought I trusted, only to find that my new friends in the area knew the potential of this person. What they didn't know was that his next victim would be an attempted homicide. Why wasn't I warned? How could they all stand around and watch as this relationship grew, knowing that I was putting myself in grave danger? Whom could I now trust? How had I not seen it coming? So many questions swirled through my mind as I spent a month staring at the walls through swollen eyes, in shock and paralysis. Looking back, I see that was the painful turning point that led to my current career and has created even more passion than I thought possible in my life.

I'd always loved working, and loved living! I had lived my life fully and with zeal. I now needed to heal so many things about myself. I didn't want that experience to hinder and destroy future relationships. Eventually I discovered that through the use of hypnosis, the *power* of healing was truly mine.

Turning my ambition, my reverence for life itself, and my dedication to heal into a career has been an extremely educational and exciting experience. After 9/11 another setback occurred. Who would have realized that the state of Utah would have been so drastically affected by the events of 9/11? Our beautiful town of Moab, with its tourist-based economy, saw the bottom fall instantly. Having been the executive director of our chamber of commerce for four and a half years, I had been asked to join a high-end international travel and adventure company, setting up the American Adventures segment, one month before the events of 9/11. Approximately one month later, I was without a job in an area where every business was wondering what would keep them afloat in this time of turmoil, especially those in the travel industry.

What was I to do now? I owned a house, land, a horse, and I had no way to keep up this lifestyle at this debilitating time. That is when everything that I had been learning and accessing to heal my own life kicked into gear. So what if I was 42 years young? I would move, go back to school, and start a new life full of meaning, helping others to move forward and improve their lives. How exciting! Was I dismayed, intimidated, a bit anxious, petrified? You bet I was! But I wanted to learn tools and strategies that would assist me in achieving my goals, so back to school I went. I re-created my life, another proof that "when one door closes, another door will open," and a much larger door at that.

Success in life and business has been achieved when you can awake in the morning knowing that your work and life are focused on assisting fellow human beings (along with yourself) to improve their mental and physical health so that they may live a more fulfilling, happy, healthy existence. To achieve that ultimate success in business, it is necessary and important to have a vision of what it is you truly desire in work and in your life. So many of us do not actually know what we want. For example, making more money is not what we want; it is the *kind of lifestyle* that comes from financial success that we need to envision in detail. When we have the ultimate vision that we can focus on, along with action, we will find that everything we do can automatically and realistically lead in the direction of that vision. Once you have that vision, believe it to *already be true* AND believe that you deserve to be successful! When you operate in this fashion, your actions are a product of your thoughts, and you are bound to succeed! One of my favorite quotes from a client handout is the following:

> *My experience is purely a product of my thought.*
> *My thought is purely a product of my decision.*
> *My decision is purely a product of my wanting.*
> *And my wanting is purely a product of my knowing.*
> —Author unknown

Business is ever changing in the world today. Consequently, learning to adapt to that change will lead to financial success. Financial success depends on your creativity, which can lead to multiple streams of income that will also allow for business expansion. Online entrepreneurship has become a popular line of work, and many brick and mortar businesses are rapidly disappearing. When expanding your business online, you may find yourself attempting to do it all on your own.

One of my projects of expansion online took way too long because I had lost sight of the fact that I am a hypnotherapist, not an expert in Internet marketing. Although I learned a lot (the hard way, I might add), had I faced the fact that I needed help from an expert in that area, I would have moved forward at a much quicker pace. In hindsight I see that I was overwhelmed, which led to spinning my wheels, which in turn caused me to achieve my goals at a much slower rate. It is very important to reinvest in your business and get the help you need so that you may continue to move forward and avoid getting stuck.

To create a business plan, I love the funnel technique. Create a vision that starts at the big end of the funnel; make it your ultimate goal, and make it big! You *can* make it happen as long as you *allow* it to happen. Another handout I give my clients is:

> The words **try, wish, and hope** need to be replaced
> with the words **can, will, and do.**

Those are important hypnotic words that need to be a big part of your vocabulary, because you want to be successful. That is your goal since you are reading this book! That's right, start with the ultimate big picture and work down from there to assess what needs to take place to make this ultimate goal your reality. Pay special attention to the word

"Allow"

That word is so important that it deserves an entire page of its own. *Allow it to happen and you will see just how easily it can happen.*

Flexibility is another important action word when it comes to growing your business and achieving your success. We live in ever-changing times, and we will see more change over the next couple of years than we ever imagined. Allow yourself to be flexible because your biggest goals could morph into greater opportunities than you ever thought possible. Although planning and action are essential, don't get overly caught up in your head as to how you are going to *make* something happen. *Allow* it to happen, believe and visualize it happening, and take action toward its happening. Unforeseen events, more often than not, will assist you. That has been my personal experience, and I am forever a child living in amazement at how much our minds, with assistance from the universe, support our exciting plans. As long as your plan is always for the betterment of others, you will succeed if you allow yourself to. Isn't this exciting?

One of my top priorities is keeping myself mentally, spiritually, and physically fit. Beginning my day with a routine that promotes this condition enables me to keep a high energy level and maintain a positive outlook on life, my goals, and the people with whom I interact throughout any given day. Don't buy into the statement "I do not have time, because I am way too busy." You may find that you are way too busy because you do not make time for this important process. Consequently, you may not be thinking as clearly as you could. In fact, you may be wasting precious time because you are failing to access the mind and body connection.

This new and beautiful phase of my life was put into motion in my early 30s, a time that cocooned and gave birth to a brand new career after I turned 40. It all began with the need for healing. If you are young, take advantage of the years you have ahead of you, and if you are experiencing your phenomenal mid-age segment of life, this is proof that you are never too old to "allow" your dreams to happen. This is also proof that it is actually possible to derive positivity out of something that was traumatic at the time.

Going back to school has become a continual stream of learning and research. Opening my hypnosis office has grown into a life of teaching and continues to grow in online programs that can reach anyone throughout the entire world. I utilize complementary techniques with hypnosis, such as Reiki, EFT, NLP, color therapy, and subliminal messaging for behavioral modification. I specialize in alcohol cessation, smoking cessation, weight loss, stress management, sports, music and speaking performance, as well as motivational and business issues.

My clients' success has everything to do with the initial education they get about hypnosis, which is imperative to their success, and they also receive a custom recorded mp3 of their sessions to reinforce achieving their important goals over a period of 30 consecutive days. My clients have a very high success rate with smoking and alcohol cessation due to the integrity of these programs and how they find themselves empowered, which is what creates *their* success. My online weight loss program has a very high success rate among my entire test group—including an 86-year-old grandmother as well as myself. You *will* succeed when the program is implemented properly from the comfort of your own home.

When people ask, How long does it take for something to manifest? I say, It takes as long as it takes for you to release the resistance. Could be 30 years, could be 40 years, could be 50, could be a week . . . could be tomorrow afternoon . . . *could be now!*

The Power Is Yours!

Biography

Julia J. Mueller

JULIA J. MUELLER is a certified hypnotist/hypnotherapist. She specializes in hypnotic coaching (also integrating other complementary techniques), assisting individuals to regain their "own" power, which leads them to achieve a healthy and abundant lifestyle and to give up habits that are cheating them of the fulfilling life they so deserve.

Julia is able to work with anyone no matter their location, due to the power of the Internet and Skype. She now lives in Sedona, Arizona, and makes trips back to her Florida location of Bonita Springs, Naples, and the Fort Myers area. Julia also offers online programs, including a proven successful 12-month weight loss program that is *very* comprehensive and reasonably priced. You can find that program at www.HypnosisForEasyWeightLoss.com. There will be many more online programs to follow. Her goal is to assist you in achieving all your desired goals no matter how near or far away you reside.

Contact Information

info@AMindandBodyConnection.com
Skype: julia.j.mueller
www.AMindandBodyConnection.com
www.HypnosisForEasyWeightLoss.com
www.juliajmueller.com

Chapter 19

Planting Seeds of Success

By Morris Nutt

My story begins on a large farm in a very small community. When people think about wide open spaces, Fontaine, Arkansas, never seems to cross their mind. Yet Fontaine was not only a great place to be from but a great place to provide a young person with an environment that taught the value of hard work, fairness, and family focus.

When you are raised in a farm family smack dab in the middle of Timbuktu and Nowhere Valley, you find out pretty quickly what you are made of and what you can handle. I must admit, for a hyperactive kid, it was mighty tough some days to stare at field after field and mile after mile of nothing but crops, dirt, and mosquitoes. And must I mention all the hard work? The shoveling, the dirt moving, the tractor driving, the walking, and the consistent grind of day in and day out physical labor, often in 100-degree heat. But hey, those were the fun parts.

Now I stare at a computer screen looking at market charts and stock quotes most of my business day, in an air-conditioned office wearing a suit and tie. The most physical part of my day is usually the small climb up a few stairs in a two-story commercial office building in the mornings. Times sure have changed. But the value system of a strong work ethic combined with a sense of treating clients fairly, treating them like family, is rooted in the furrows gently plowed while growing up in Fontaine.

The greatest success tip for today's economy that I can offer others who are truly open to listening would be three simple words: *Focus, Patience, and*

Perseverance. In a society of instant gratification, multitasking, and a huge lack of commitment, these three words have never been more important to understand or rung more true. It seems the core challenge today is to have a singular focus, the patience to allow things to work themselves out, and the perseverance to not pull a move from the *Pirates of the Caribbean* movie and "Abandon Ship!"

I define success as the ability to help others in such a way that you can't help but be helped too. The value you bring to others should be so great that it would be impossible for you or your services to be ignored. It is through this process that success flows naturally, like a stream cutting through dirt and rock on its way to level ground. Need proof? Think about this for a moment. How many people do you feed throughout the year? It may seem an odd question, but really think about it for a while. If you are a single person, then you more than likely are just working to feed yourself. If you are the bread-winner in a household, you may be feeding two to ten people. On average it is probably just three or four people, including you.

Now let's think about the American farmer. How many people do you think he or she feeds in a year? The answer is 155 people. Because of the efficiency of our American farmers, we spend only 10% of our disposable income on food, unlike Pakistan, whose citizens spend 50%; Jordan, where they spend 43%; or Chinese citizens, who spend 32%. So who provides more value? It seems like an unfair question. Farmers naturally feed people as part of their job, while you and I (outside our immediate family) do not. But the facts remain, the farmer provides an overwhelming amount of additional value compared to the typical worker. Because of this fact, farmers have solidified their place in the economic chain. They are rewarded in today's environment because of this extreme value.

Look at your industry and job and recognize the value you can bring forth. Is it happening? Are you justifying your position? Are you truly a force that others can't do without? If you are, then keep up the great work! We need more people like you. If not, then let's lay out some steps for you to help others greatly and help yourself in the process.

You have to find your way.

Albert Einstein possibly summed up success best when he said, "Try not to become a person of success but a person of value." This quote leads us to the first step for you to create your own success:

Focus—If I were to hand you a single strand of fiber and ask if you could break it, tear it, or pull it apart, you would more than likely be able to perform the task rather easily with just your bare hands. However, if I were to take 500 strands of fiber and weave them together in such a way that they formed a piece of rope fairly large in diameter, could you then break it, tear it, or pull it apart using only your bare hands? Probably not. This example is focus in its simplest form.

Each of us has thousands of thoughts throughout the day. Most of those thoughts get lonely and leave us. If our thoughts are scattered, if they are singular in nature, they will not hold up to being lost, dropped, broken, or torn apart. Imagine your day if you were truly focused. If you weren't attempting to juggle all those thoughts, all those email boxes, all those small details, what would your day look like then? How much more successful and happy would you be knowing you had complete clarity and lots of energy to apply toward meeting that focused objective? If those thoughts become intertwined and melted together to form a singular focus, they can be the seeds of some of the greatest ideas ever born. Edison's light bulb invention is such a great example of singular focus and mission. Thomas Edison, as most have read, attempted to get the light bulb to work more than 10,000 times to no avail. On his last attempt, it worked! Edison later lamented, "I didn't fail 10,000 times. I just found 10,000 ways a light bulb wouldn't work." But Edison did find the one way eventually because he had supreme singular FOCUS. He also possessed the next two seeds of success.

Patience—Many times in life, we know what we want—we may even know how to go about getting it—but then we fail to achieve the goal. Why? One of the biggest reasons for failure to achieve a goal is simply our lack of patience to stick with it long enough for success to happen. Perhaps we simply underestimate how long it should take to achieve the goal at hand. The mind can certainly play tricks on us. We can fake ourselves out of the ballgame. How many times do players quit a team due to a perceived lack of playing time, only later to find out they were merely seconds away from being named the starter? We also learn from Edison through all his trials and errors that he never gave up. Yes, he was focused. He was also willing to continue to be patient with himself and the process until he found the way.

It is easy to confuse patience with perseverance and commitment. I believe that patience is your ability to allow things to happen the way they are supposed to happen without allowing yourself to be knocked off course because of timing. For example, if you tell me you are going to meet me for lunch at noon, and I know you are a person of your word, I will wait for you to arrive even if you are running several minutes late. Some may not agree and get back into their cars and drive off after 15 or so minutes because they feel their time is so valuable. However, if I am willing to schedule a lunch time with you, it benefits me to stay the course and wait for you to show, even if you are a few minutes late. This way we still meet and accomplish what we set out to do. Far too often today, people feel so rushed, so pushed for time, that they truly fail to see the value in slowing down and allowing things to just be. We all from time to time need to stand still and just be. Patience allows us to marinate and have a more flavorful life.

Most often, you will gain more in reality than you lose in perception by simply staying the course.

Perseverance—Commitment and perseverance are interchangeable words to me. If you are committed to a cause or a goal, then you automatically persevere until you have accomplished the task. One of my great role models was my father. I have probably spent more hours one-on-one with that man when I was a child, a young adult, and a man than with any other person. Of course he would rub off on me like mud sticks to a tractor wheel.

When we think about our role models, we think about people who possessed certain traits we admired, honored, and imitated. My father, while not degreed from a university, had a doctorate from the School of Hard Knocks. With that knowledge and experience and a School of Life diploma, he was able to impart to me one of the greatest of skills for achieving success— the ability to look doubt and fear squarely in the eye and keep moving forward, the ability to persevere.

If this area has held you back from your success, let's talk about why and how you can learn to persevere moving forward. As I mentioned earlier, as a child I was hyperactive. I lacked focus. I had no patience and I absolutely had no idea how to persevere. When it got hot in the kitchen, I was the first to want out. Even the first time I heard the word, "perseverance," from my father, I was like a contestant on *Wheel of Fortune* asking, "Can I buy a vowel?" The word not only meant something harder than usual. It even sounded hard.

My dad didn't let me off the hook, though, and you should not let yourself off the hook either. I will explain to you as my father explained to me, "When the going gets tough, the tough get going!" My dad hated idle time like Subway despises grams of fat. He believed that the true measure of a person was discovered during the heat of the battle, when the sledding got tough, when you wanted to quit—how you would then react to the adversity. Would you tuck your tail and slink away in defeat or would you *persevere*? So, Vanna, what's it going to be? How do I solve this puzzle?

Edison handled it by looking for another way without giving up. He had focus, he allowed himself time (patience), but he didn't give up. He merely tried another way (perseverance). My dad taught this to me as well. He would say, "Son, either you know you are right and you keep doing it over and over until you succeed or you know you might need to keep going but use a different technique. It's one or the other. It's that simple."

I would encourage you to apply this belief to the perseverance portion of your life. Instead of getting caught up in society's lack of attention span and lack of commitment, persevere! Keep trying until you succeed. If you become convinced you need to try another way of achieving the goal, go ahead. But whatever you do, do not give up; keep moving forward. It's that simple.

I do hope that these three seedlings of success find a fertile place within you and take root. With proper care and lots of good thoughts, your harvest will be more than bountiful, and you too will feed hundreds of people with your offerings.

God Bless,

Morris

Biography

Morris Nutt

MORRIS NUTT is an author, a speaker, a consultant, a thought leader, and a wealth mindset expert living in Memphis, Tennessee. He is CEO of Morris Nutt Financial, LLC. Morris enjoys traveling, reading, speaking, and writing. He especially enjoys helping others achieve their most worthy goals and spending time with his family.

Morris is co-author of *The Laws of Financial Success,* with Edward Cowles, and one of the contributing authors in the new best seller from Brian Tracy, *Counter-Attack.* He currently has three other books in the creation process. Morris is a member of the National Academy of Best-Selling Authors and a 2011 recipient of the Golden Quill, an award given to authors who have achieved best-selling status. Morris enjoys helping others. His motto is, "You are destined for greatness!" For more information about Morris, visit www.thelawsoffinancialsuccess.com or morrisnuttfinancial.com.

Contact Information

901-484-8726
www.thelawsoffinancialsuccess.com
www.morrisnuttfinancial.com

Chapter 20

Say Goodbye to Constraints and Hello to Success

By Kevin B. O'Connor

"*H*oney, I made over $10,000 this month!*" I could finally look my wife in the eyes and tell her everything was going to be okay. Just a few months prior I had been on the verge of filing for bankruptcy. In 1990 I cofounded a manufacturing company. We were soon doing millions in annual revenue. By 1997 I was in financial ruin. I knew that a J.O.B. was not going to get me out of the hole I was in. The story begins in Jamaica. The year is 1995.

"I've been diagnosed with a brain tumor. I'm going back to England." Those were the words that my head of manufacturing told me a week before catching a plane from Kingston, Jamaica, home to London. Of course I was totally blown away for David. He was in his early 30s, full of energy, and very experienced in apparel manufacturing. In the midst of my sadness for him was a rising panic. We were just six months into a multimillion-dollar contract with Fruit of the Loom. We were leveraged up to our eyeballs, with hundreds of thousands of dollars invested in our new factory, and there was a lot of fine print in our contract. *We had to perform.*

Problem: It is not easy finding experienced top-level management in Jamaica, just like it's not easy finding leaders in your networking business. I knew nothing about running a factory. I knew how to run a business. I knew how to bring in sales; the factory was booked solid for three years. Overnight

I went from the boss upstairs in the air-conditioned office to a grunt over-seeing the assembly line. There was one problem: *I was completely clueless.*

It was like getting in the ring with Mike Tyson. I didn't stand a chance.

Luckily, I had been studying two books: *The Goal* and *It's Not Luck*, by Eli Goldratt (two of the best network marketing books that are not about network marketing). Like a great detective novel, these books unravel the mystery of the theory of constraints.

"What the heck are you talking about?" you might wonder. What does any of this have to do with network marketing or Internet marketing?

Little did I know that this crisis would lay the foundation for network marketing success. But before that happened, I would have to beat the crap out of my proverbial Mike Tyson.

I soon discovered that the factory was really a disaster. There were under-lying issues that were about to kick us in the, well, I'll keep it clean, but we were in trouble. Using the "in the ring with Tyson" analogy, I knew that if I didn't move fast, he was going to knock me out. We would not meet our contract requirements, and we would have hell to pay.

The theory of constraints taught me a logical sequence to turn the factory around, to push the bottlenecks forward and to eventually break the bottlenecks. We turned it around. We were meeting our deliveries. *But none of it mattered.* We found out too late that Fruit of the Loom had opened factories in Mexico and El Salvador. They yanked our contract, we had no other customers, and we were bleeding cash and could not fight back. In short, we sold the factory at a fire sale price, and *I was knocking on the door of bankruptcy.*

So there I was, running an apparel assembly line, even though I don't know how to turn on a sewing machine. Not good. But I'm seeing through new eyes as I learn to implement the theory of constraints. This would be the key to my success in network marketing; I just didn't know it at the time.

You're driving down the road and all of a sudden you are in bumper-to-bumper traffic. As you go farther along, you realize that two or three lanes are squeezing into one. This is a constraint known as a bottleneck. About 10 cars ahead you see the construction crew remove the barriers, and suddenly all the cars sail through. The bottleneck has been removed.

Factories frequently experience specific bottlenecks. So do businesses. Bottlenecks occur because of constraints. A constraint is anything that can cause production to stop or slow down. A constraint is the cause; the bottleneck is the result.

Let me describe our production line. We made boxer shorts. There were only seven steps, seemingly simple, but the complexities of moving one piece of fabric down an assembly line and have it come out as a boxer short are amazingly complex. Having a new associate join you and move down the assembly line of becoming a successful and profitable distributor is even more complex, and just as in a factory, anything can go wrong.

A constraint in my factory could be a machine down, two or three people on an operation out of work that day, the wrong color thread going on the machines, and the list goes on and on. These are constraining the flow of goods from the first operation to the last operation. When the constraints happen at the first few operations, they create a huge bottleneck with hardly anything getting to the finish line, and *nothing at the finish line equals no money.*

What I learned was that I had to remove and control the constraints at the first operation so that more could flow to the second. As the constraints were removed, the production line would send more goods faster to the end of the line. It's called "breaking the bottleneck."

To break the bottleneck, you have to move the bottleneck forward. You want the bottleneck to be near the last operation. If the constraints and the bottlenecks are all at the first few operations everything shuts down. When it is near the last operation, it is close to completion, almost a finished product, in a wonderful state of "almostness," and it is easy to focus on it and move it to completion.

Fast forward to 1997. I had to do something fast. I knew that people had made big money in network marketing and that I could start for next to no money. I realized that the theory of constraints applied to network marketing. A new networker has the constraint of fear; the constraint of a skeptical spouse, friend, family member; the constraint of a lack of knowledge and confidence. Not knowing that there are constraints and how to identify them in yourself or in your team will cause bottlenecks. When the bottlenecks happen in the early days of a new distributor, everything piles up; they get frustrated and often quit.

We have all kinds of cute sayings in MLM: "If your why is big enough you'll figure out how" is a common one. You can add your own here, but sayings will not break a bottleneck unless the distributor is close to the finish line and in a state of "almostness." What the heck does that mean? It means that they must experience some success before their belief system is ready to push them the rest of the way. You, as leader/mentor/upline, need to help them identify and remove those early constraints so that they are moving toward completion.

What is true, and has never changed, is that your associates must bring desire. Without desire new associates are wasting your time. They *will* become a constraint in your business and frustrate you. Distributors without desire are on their way to quitting, and the sooner you know this, the more you can focus on those who want to succeed. Seems basic, right? It can be, but only if *you learn how to identify your constraints and move the bottleneck forward.*

What I'm talking about applies to any business, and to your personal life. Here's my formula for breaking the bottleneck:

Write down every constraint that is keeping you from reaching a specific goal. (It doesn't matter if it's an income goal, a weight loss goal, a relationship goal, etc.)

*It is critical that you write down **every** constraint. This is an exercise in uncovering anything and everything that creates a bottleneck to achieving your goal. This includes emotions, mental blocks, fears, and so on.*

Rank them in the order of difficulty that they currently cause you.

*Choose the **hardest** on the list and the **easiest** on the list.*

*Make an action plan to resolve the hardest and the easiest along with an accompanying time table. **Do not** move on to any of the other issues until these are resolved. You will find that by the time you resolve the top one to three issues that the rest of the list was interconnected to these and will no longer be constraints.*

*It is critical that you act on the **hardest** and the **easiest** simultaneously. The hardest will usually create fear and resistance from you, and the easiest will help give a sense of accomplishment and balance.*

When I was on the verge of bankruptcy, my wife wanted me to get a job. Security is important to her. It was a reasonable request under the circumstances, but I would never have been able to get out of the financial mess I was in if I had done that. This was my *hardest* constraint. I made an action plan that I negotiated with her; if I accomplished x amount of income in x amount of time, she would agree to the next time period. This removed the immediate constraint and gave me very strict targets to shoot for. The *easiest* was designing and printing business cards. It felt great getting that little thing accomplished.

As I identified and removed constraints, my check went up. Within 10 months, I was debt free. I concentrated on teaching my team how to remove constraints until my organization was largely free of bottlenecks, and several employees became five-figure monthly earners. The bottleneck on my income was disappearing as I climbed into the $20,000, $30,000, $40,000-plus per month club.

You can only live a life without constraints when you learn how to identify and eliminate them. I wish you success on your path to freedom.

Biography

Kevin B. O'Connor

From performing at Carnegie Hall to running a factory in Kingston, Jamaica; from crushing debt to top-earning global network marketing leader, KEVIN O'CONNOR's adventures in life and business have made him a dynamic speaker, leader, and coach. His hard-won "Lessons from the Factory Floor" provide a systematic approach to success and profit for your home-based business.

Contact Information

215-233-2103
kevin@kevinboconnor.com
www.kevinboconnor.com

Chapter 21

Unleash the Alpha Wolf Inside Your Mind

LIVE THE ABUNDANT LIFE
YOU WERE DESTINED TO LIVE

By Chuck Gray

When you unleash the alpha wolf inside your mind, you become free to live the abundant life you were meant to live. The alpha wolf does not just survive. The alpha wolf truly lives a meaningful life. The alpha wolf is the leader of the pack, getting what he wants because he is respected for being dominant, self-confident, and trustworthy. The alpha is respected because others know that they can count on him. Please also understand that this is all equally true for either the alpha male or the alpha female.

Understanding the natural instincts of wolves and relating them to your human experience can be your key to happiness, personal fulfillment, and prosperity. What lessons can we learn from the wolf pack? We will take a quick look at the natural alpha wolf and the wolf pack to see what attributes we can emulate in our lives. The studies conducted of wolves in Yellowstone and other "wolf parks" in recent years have produced some surprising revelations.

A wolf pack consists of an alpha male and an alpha female, their pups, sometimes the alpha pair's brothers or sisters, and occasionally an unrelated lone wolf who was accepted into the pack by demonstrating submissive behavior. Wolves are very intelligent. They are much more intelligent than dogs and have a brain that is one-third larger than that of a dog. Wolves quickly become bored if they are not being intellectually stimulated. They form deeper bonds of love with each other than what a dog is capable of experiencing.

The alpha pair is dominant over the rest of the pack, but they are equal to each other and divide up the family responsibilities. All the females in the pack have to answer to the alpha female, and all the males in the pack have to answer to the alpha male. The alpha male leads the hunt and defends the territory while the alpha female makes the most critical decision of where to live and maintains the home front. This den site must have enough prey in the area to support the pack, so she has to make a good choice for the pack to thrive.

These two alpha wolves are the only ones in the pack that are allowed to breed. The other pack members are subordinates who respect the alpha's dominance and intelligent decisions. The attributes of the alpha wolf include leadership skills, decisiveness, confidence, charisma, and a thorough understanding of body language. Alpha wolves are not mean or cruel. They are leaders and have the cooperation of the pack to accomplish great things that could not be done as a lone wolf. For example, hunting big game is possible when you are leading a team.

The alpha wolf does not dominate by brute force alone; in fact, the beta wolf, or second in command, may be much bigger and stronger and act as the alpha's bodyguard or enforcer in the pack. The alpha wolf may not be the strongest, fastest, or even the smartest. Achieving high rank depends more on projecting an attitude of self-confidence. This is a critical lesson for us to learn, that it is your attitude, your attitude, your attitude that will determine your ultimate success or failure in all aspects of your life.

Wolves love to work and play. It is all the same to them! Hollywood movies and even documentaries mistakenly show wolves acting mean and snarling at their prey. In fact, they are joyful and have a great time on the hunt, wagging their tails. They only snarl or growl when they are about to fight another wolf. Wolves avoid fighting bears or humans, preferring to just avoid them. The prey is their food. A wolf snarling at an elk would be like you being angry at the slice of apple pie you are about to eat!

The alpha wolf is in charge and has a lot of responsibility and daily decisions to make, but the alpha also enjoys the privilege of having a world of choices. The alphas eat their fill, but will make sure the pups are fed and not abused by the other adult wolves. Taking on the mantle of being the alpha wolf is a conscious life-changing decision. The alpha is a leader, teacher, protector, mentor, and role model. Many wolves never become alpha. Their lives will revolve around the decisions made by the alpha wolf. The non-alpha does not mate, eats leftovers, and spends his or her days kowtowing to those more dominant.

An adult wolf must make the momentous decision to be an alpha wolf and set out on this epic journey or take the easier road of settling for a lesser life position in the pack, which is like adults deciding to live in their parents' basement. An intelligent wolf may leave to search for a mate and start his own pack, taking the lessons learned from alpha mom and dad with him. How self-confident that individual must be to leave the security of the pack and go off on this perilous adventure to create his own destiny!

The first attribute of the alpha wolf is decisiveness. You have to make the important decision to be an alpha wolf, and then you have to take action to achieve that status. Decisiveness is an attractive and important quality to dominate or lead others. When something happens, be the one in the group who steps up and takes charge. Make a decision. Even in small matters such as where to go to eat, don't ever say, "I don't know. Where do you want to go? What do you want to do?" That just drives people crazy (especially the opposite sex), and your social position and status suffer. Decide fast. It is much better to make a bad decision and fail than to pussyfoot around. Being consistently decisive even in small matters is charismatic, and your perceived status will soar.

The alpha wolf is the leader of the pack because he has the self-confidence and dominant behavior that others can't help but respect. He takes control when situations call for a decision maker to reign in the chaos. Flying off the handle or blowing off steam when things are not going your way is not attractive and is a self-sabotaging beta move. Throwing a fit of anger over frustrating situations just makes you look like a fool. An alpha wolf has self-control, including the ability to do nothing when restraint is called for. Self-control is being cool when the world around you is going crazy. Take action when it is appropriate. Learn the skills needed for the task at hand. Competence produces a calming state of confidence, allowing you to achieve a high level of productivity when those who have less competence are panicking. Handling situations with finesse and calm leadership is an alpha trait, while being an aggressive arrogant jerk, pushing others around, is a beta trait that loses for you in the long run.

The alpha wolf is an early riser and does not sleep in even on the weekend. He wakes, stretches, and gets active. As Benjamin Franklin said, "Early to bed and early to rise makes a man healthy, wealthy and wise." All successful people are early risers. Have an alpha morning routine.

My morning consists of a few minutes of yoga to get the kinks out. Then every other morning I lift weights for just a few more minutes to strengthen and tone. I make my bed while the coffee is brewing. During the day, simply seeing my bed made gives me the satisfying feeling of being organized and uncluttered, which is psychologically uplifting. Making your bed only takes a minute or less and it sets the tone for the day.

The alpha wolf is clean, healthy, and majestic in appearance, which is immediately recognized by all. In short, in my best Billy Crystal voice, "He looks marvelous, and it is better to look good than to feel good."

Always dress as the alpha wolf, because that is who you are. Don't just look like an alpha wolf. Be the alpha wolf. In business or formal situations, be the best dressed one there. Remember you are the alpha wolf in your life. Everyone else is in your reality now. Wear what is appropriate for the occasion or location. Think style and class. Wear quality fabric that is clean and sharp. Women have lots of choices with colorful business suits, dresses, and jewelry.

Men would be well advised to stick to blue tailored suits for the top alpha look. IBM has thoroughly researched color and status, and their salesmen are only allowed to wear blue suits. The style and quality of the shoes you are wearing can make or break you when interacting with a woman. You can drive up in a Maserati, but if she sees that your shoes are scuffed, she will assume that your life is unkempt and you'll lose her respect.

The tie is one of the most important aspects of dress that influences how others view your status because it is a symbol of respectability and responsibility. Stick with 100% silk ties and wear them at the correct length. The tip of the tied tie should just touch the top of your belt buckle. Don't wear it too short like Oliver Hardy or too long so it is down by your fly like Stan Laurel.

Smell good, but too much cologne is a beta move, and you will lose respect. Keep jewelry to a minimum. Women do not trust men who wear pinky rings for some reason I can't fathom, but that is what several have told me. I usually wear a tie tack made from a coin because it generates lots of comments and has become my trademark. A quality watch, cufflinks, tie tack, and a ring should be about the extent of an alpha wolf's bling. Never underestimate the power of quality over quantity. An expensive pen is the alpha wolf's sword. If you use a briefcase or portfolio, buy the best you can afford. Look successful and you will be successful, because you will attract people to you. Everyone wants to be associated with winners, so look like a winner and you will win.

What if you happen to see an NFL football coach somewhere, like in a store shopping, in his casual clothes? How would you expect this respected successful person to dress in a casual setting? I imagine he would be wearing a pair of nice-looking comfortable casual slacks and a 100% top quality cotton sport shirt. You would be shocked if he was wearing an old worn faded shirt or dingy sneakers. Wear the clothes that are appropriate for the venue, but look the part of the alpha wolf at work and at play. Remember that all the world is a stage. Claim the part of the alpha wolf for yourself. You will not be crowned the alpha wolf. You must look the part, act the part, and become the part from the inside out or from the outside in, but like Napoleon, you must crown yourself the alpha wolf.

When you are self-confident and secure in the fact that you have high value, your special inner quality will drive you forward with the persistence to get what you want and where you want to go. You will inspire others to trust you as they feel you are genuine. Unleashing the alpha wolf inside your mind requires a powerful belief in yourself. The alpha wolf does not project insecurity in any aspect of his body language.

Stand up and imagine you are in front of an audience about to begin a lecture on the attributes of the alpha wolf. Now imagine that standing directly in front of you is your future you, who has fully embodied the self-confident nature of the alpha wolf. This future you is successfully entertaining the audience with his or her charismatic personality. Picture your future you for a minute or two. Notice the powerful posture and grace. Now step forward into your future you and fuse together. Smile and feel the power. It feels good to be the alpha wolf!

There is no law that you must be poor or that you can't improve all aspects of your life. No one can make you be less than who you want to be. Don't just work hard all your life to keep the wolf from the door. Decide to be the alpha wolf.

Biography

Chuck Gray

CHUCK GRAY received his bachelor's degree from the University of Dayton and is a 2011 graduate of The American College. He has 20 years' experience in the insurance industry, is an Alpha Wolf Society founding member, a certified RetireSure Advisor, and treasurer of the Wayne Lakes Booster Club.

Contact Information

937-239-6268
PO Box 432
Greenville, OH 45331
ChuckGray@live.com
www.thealphawolf.com
www.chuckgrayonline.com

Chapter 22

Success vs. Significance

By Gail B. Blackburn

*M*any consider those two words to be one and the same. I know I did in my "previous life." Before I had a family, the only thing that mattered to me was to work hard on my career and to make money. Like many, I scurried through life with blinders on, not taking much time to help my fellow man.

I definitely reaped the financial rewards of a workaholic lifestyle—I had an amazing career and made fantastic money in my late 20s and early 30s as a project manager and computer modeler for a world-renowned hydrologist in his 70s. He was all about science—a true genius. I was all about art and creativity—very much not the genius! My talents lay in perfecting the balance between art and science, and bridging the gap between a genius and the rest of us for litigation in ground water contamination. I loved my job and considered myself quite the "success" financially.

Life was great—I was a single homeowner with a nice car and plenty of money to play with! Then something, or should I say someone, came in and started to stir up the pot. This guy in my complex kept bugging me to go out with him, and the more I said no, the more he persisted. Eventually I decided that a break in scenery from working with a 70-year-old might be nice and agreed to go out. Three years later, Bret and I were married in the Bahamas and soon after bought a larger home. Still carefree, we constantly dined out and literally lived for the day, not thinking much about, or preparing for, the future.

But then you get to a point where something's missing. Every year we were blessed to have Bret's son, Bryan, from his first marriage spend the summer with us. And the end of each summer left us devastated upon his departure back to his mother. So we decided to add to our family. Little did I know what God had in store for me . . . infertility surgery and treatments and a high-risk pregnancy taught me discipline, patience, and the real value of human life. I would no longer take for granted what most couples do—the ability to bear children.

Armed with my new traits, I still wanted to work hard on my career and make tons of money. So much so that I was working 60 hours a week until the day I learned I would need an emergency C-section to save our baby. You see, I knew the baby was breech, but I kept putting off the hospital procedure to turn her around because I had a very important deadline at work. Had my boss known what was going on, I have no doubt he would have sent me to the hospital immediately, but I thought I could handle it—and besides, work was really important. When I did finally go in, they discovered that she had less than a teaspoon of amniotic fluid left and took her immediately. I really beat myself up about that one—had we waited one day longer we would have lost her. . . . That taught me about divine intervention and gave me complete faith in God.

As I fell more and more in love with my daughter every day, my original thoughts of day care after one month were modified to three months. After a month, my boss suggested I work half time at home and bring Britney into the office with me half time. I quickly accepted his most generous offer. Then at three months we learned Britney had hydrocephalus (fluid on the brain) and needed immediate brain surgery, and three days later we learned she had achondroplasia (a form of dwarfism).

Before my daughter, I never understood the true meaning of unconditional love. Her birth difference just made me love her all the more, and nothing in the world mattered but her health and well being. I decided to put my career on hold and concentrate all my efforts on my most precious gift from heaven above.

Talk about a major transition—from living large on two salaries to squeaking by on one. I never thought we could do it, but we did, simply by cutting out all the little extravagances that really don't matter in the end. I loved being a stay-at-home mom and took advantage of that time to research everything I could on her birth differences. We became heavily involved in the support group Little People of America, and our eyes were opened to a new and wonderful world.

It didn't take very long for me to dive into volunteering for our local chapter. I absolutely fell in love with the world of volunteerism. Yes, it is an unpaid job, but no amount of money can give you the warm fuzzy feeling that you get from helping another. Volunteerism can give you the highest of highs when a person tells you what a difference you have made in their lives.

I think most people define success by how much money they make. If you think about it along those terms, success is completely subjective. You could have both a minimum-wage earner and a CEO feel they are equally successful! I consider my husband to be extremely successful. When I first met him, I found it intriguing that whenever I thought I knew him, he would throw me for a loop and keep me guessing. Looking back, I now realize that, as weird as it sounds, I fell in love with his brain injury. See, Bret sustained a traumatic brain injury (TBI) back in the Army in 1985. He literally lost everything . . . his career, his wife and newborn baby, everything. When I look back on his medical records, it astounds me that he was told he would never be able to have a job, a family, anything. Thank God this amazing man didn't let anything the outside world had to say lessen his inner resolve. That is the epitome of success in my book.

Over the years, the lingering effects of Bret's TBI worsened, and he found it hard to maintain steady employment. So we decided to make the bold move into self-employment and started a handyman business (the first year with partners, then on our own). Over the years we built an extremely successful business solely on word of mouth—Bret doing the physical labor and me doing all the paperwork from home while raising Britney. It was the perfect solution, and when you are honest, caring, and fair, word spreads like wildfire. I hated turning clients away, and little did I know at the time, but the stress manifested itself in Bret through an onslaught of many physical injuries. I now had my very own "Tim the Tool Man Taylor" living under my roof, but he had to take matters a bit further by getting permanently assigned parking at the emergency room (at least it felt that way)!

There comes a time when everyone breaks, and Bret's time was in December 2004 when he was putting up holiday lights for a client and fell off a two-story roof. This time assigned parking wasn't needed as he was the recipient of an exclusive helicopter ride. That's when I learned the sobering odds of having a second TBI after the initial one.

So now what? "No income" doesn't go very far in any economy! I didn't really see myself going back to the corporate world as Britney had many surgeries under her belt by this time, and I didn't want to overwhelm Bret by asking him to take care of her all alone and also deal with his own stuff. I know that God knew my plans long before I did. In the same week that Bret had his TBI, a friend of mine who was also a little person, Mark Trombino, had his world turned upside down on a larger scale than I had. His wife was in a head-on car collision coming home from work, instantly became a "mini Christopher Reeve," with high-level spinal cord injuries, and eventually passed away. Instead of dwelling on my own problems, I coordinated a fundraising carwash and so forth for their family. It was much easier for me to focus on someone else.

Here we were—two families where the major breadwinner was out of commission and the stay-at-home parent was left wondering what the heck to do next. I had been volunteering in Florida for another friend who was a little person, with his bully program, and became quite knowledgeable on the subject. In the meantime, Mark was beginning to share his own story. It seemed only natural for the two of us to partner up, so we co-founded our now nonprofit Motivational Small Talk.

Over the years we have made an incredible impact on the lives of students of all ages with our presentations on bullying and teaching them not simply to tolerate the differences we all have but to truly embrace them. We have also presented at many corporations, religious institutions, and so forth on diversity awareness, disability education, and helping others to overcome obstacles. Mark is the "up front" man doing the presenting, while I am the "behind the scenes" gal doing research and development, speech writing, PowerPoint assemblage, and website development. I am finally growing my own voice as well and have presented on social networking and Internet safety for families among other topics. My goal is to inspire other spouses of TBI survivors, and to help parents empower their "differently abled" children.

It's not about the money for us. It's about how many lives we can touch with our unique messages. Daily headlines on "bullycide" and school shootings only fuel our passion to empower victims everywhere. God has a plan, and we both feel so blessed to be living ours.

I revel every day as I watch my beautiful 14-year-old daughter's determination and self-reliance, which she demonstrated at an incredibly young age. Infuriating at times? Definitely! But what teenager isn't, right? I am so blessed to have such an amazing role model in my life. Britney doesn't let anything or anyone get her down. She is my rock.

Both Britney's birth difference and Bret's brain injury have been blessings beyond measure to me. They have helped me grow into the person I was meant to be and have taught me the true meaning of success—to live a life of significance through service.

Biography

Gail B. Blackburn

GAIL BLACKBURN is a wife, a mother, and an entrepreneur whose background consists of art, graphics, computers, business, and project management. She has a BS in business management and is co-founder of the nonprofit Motivational Small Talk, Inc. Gail also enjoys volunteering for Little People of America, Gilbert Presbyterian Church, and the East Valley Youth Symphony.

Contact Information

www.GailBlackburn.com
Gail@GailBlackburn.com
Facebook.com/GailBBlackburn
www.MotivationalSmallTalk.org
phone/fax: 480-926-0608

Chapter 23
A Well-Conditioned Mind

By Edward Brown

*I*t was the summer of 1982.

The play-off game, my last year of little league.

I was 13 years old, and my uncle had just passed away. . . .

I stood at the plate, bases loaded, with two outs, full count—three balls, two strikes. This was my opportunity to hit the winning run. This would be for my uncle. I would be the game-winning hero. This is the very moment many people end up facing as they lay everything on the line to create their own success in life. It comes to that moment of truth that will make or break an individual in business.

As the pitcher wound up, I began thinking that maybe he would pitch me a ball. After all, my uncle's spirit was with me, the gods were shining on me, the universe was going to give me the success I desired and deserved with minimal effort on my part. The ball left the pitcher's hand. Everything was happening so fast. It was crunch time, and I needed to make a decision, but I was unprepared. The ball was there. I reacted, swinging the bat, and the umpire yelled strike three. The game was over.

How did this happen to me?

Anyone else would have hit a homerun.

It didn't make sense. I was a good ball player.

When we played neighborhood ball, I would always get on base and even hit homeruns.

157

This pattern would follow me throughout the better part of my life. Every time I was in my comfort zone, I would shine, but when it came to the important moments in life, I crumbled under pressure. During class I had all the answers until the test, which I would usually fail. Girls were fond of me, I was cute and funny, but I had no girlfriend. I had good job opportunities and started a few businesses, some that did better than others, but none that challenged me, fulfilled me, or created the success I desired. I was rambling through life simply reacting to the circumstances life presented me.

Why does this always happen to me?

It was nearly 20 years later, when I was walking with a friend I could count on to listen and provide good advice, that I received an unexpected rude awakening. He explained to me that as a friend, he was willing to listen to me if I wanted to continue making excuses and blaming random circumstances in my life for all my problems. He then said, I am not trying to insult you, but everyone has problems; everyone has failures. We had stopped walking, and my friend placed his hand on my shoulder, as he often did when he wanted to share a piece of heart-felt advice. He looked me directly in the eyes and said: My question to you is, are you going to continue to blame others while you watch all the good people around you disappear because they are tired of hearing all the negativity, or are you going to stop reacting to what life is handing you and learn how to take a proactive approach in obtaining what you want out of life? That was a moment of realization for me.

Deep down I knew he was right. It was an ugly truth about myself that my friend had just unveiled to me. I felt relieved knowing I was now ready to become accountable for my own actions and confront life head on. He knew he now had my undivided attention, as it was one of those rare moments when I was actually doing all the listening. He related to my situation by explaining that years ago, he had worked on his own personal development skills by reading books, listening to audios, and attending seminars in an effort to improve his sales and public speaking ability. This process had led him to recognize the value in networking with other like-minded individuals.

My friend then shared an enjoyable method of obtaining advice from others. It simply involves asking someone for a moment of their time to answer a few questions about their areas of expertise. This technique works wonderfully, because once you respect people, show initiative, and allow them the opportunity to feel their opinion is valued, they are generally happy to share their real-life knowledge with you, as my friend was now doing for me. That evening I obtained one of those books, started to read, became so intrigued that I stayed up all night to finish the book, and from that day forward my life began to change. What I needed to do was clear.

Set Goals—Take Action—Stay Focused

I have remained determined to succeed throughout all the struggles life has thrown at me. I refuse to give up my dreams. This is a very important characteristic for any goal-oriented individual to possess. Most people give up when it seems like life has knocked them down one too many times. This is unfortunate because usually at this point in life, when most people give up, success is right around the corner. I have no intention of giving up. It is my will to succeed in life.

Achieving success begins with establishing a goal, taking action, and remaining focused on achieving your goal. This requires a certain amount of determination, persistence, and a strong will to succeed.

A person's plans fail when . . .
A person fails to have a plan.

Throughout my life I had enjoyed exercising and conditioning my body. Now I was going to exercise and condition my mind to prepare for the challenges I would face while achieving my goals. Over the next five years I continued to educate myself, invest in my future, and condition my mind for success. Today, when I step up to the plate in life, when the bases are loaded and I have a full count, I am no longer looking for life to hand me the win. I no longer operate in a reactive manner to what life throws at me. I take a proactive approach so I am prepared before I step up to the plate. I have conditioned myself not to go for the homerun but to concentrate on obtaining many consistent base hits. Many consistent successes will create a solid foundation that adds up over time.

When you implement a proactive system, you will experience steady growth, and an occasional strikeout won't make or break you or your business. A proactive system involves constant conditioning, continued education with advanced training techniques, and staying up to date within your market. This keeps your mind sharp so that when the right opportunity presents itself, you have the ability and confidence required to hit an occasional homerun anyway.

You have the strength and ability to make these changes within yourself.

Action Step: Start a journal, writing down your goals for today, one week from now, a month, a year, and then where you would like to see yourself five years from today.

Now take action!

You have already made a wise decision by choosing to read this today, so remember, I am always here to assist you with any sticking points you may have along the way.

Serve Others

Conditioning my mind helped me discover that the best way to create my own success was to improve my ability to serve others. I immediately felt qualified in this area because as a blue collar worker, I had plenty of experience being a servant of others. I was also pleasantly surprised to learn that some of the most successful people develop a similar characteristic. Early in their careers, they were some of the best servants of others. In the end it comes down to this: The more people you are able to assist with obtaining what they want, need, or desire in life, the better the chance of achieving your own success.

Develop a Plan and a Brand

I studied various aspects of businesses and noticed that many of the most successful business had something in common. They had a plan! Many of these companies operate successfully in different locations around the world because they have developed a system. These companies were also exceptional at creating, establishing, and marketing a brand.

I needed a plan.
I needed to develop a system.
I needed to create, establish, and market my brand.

These are such simple and often overlooked concepts, but they are extremely important factors for anyone interested in creating their own success in any type of business.

I implemented this knowledge to create my own success within my construction business. Throughout this process, people began to recognize how more experienced business owners were struggling within the construction industry while I had started with nothing and begun to thrive in such a short time. I experienced consistent growth in my business each year, which was being noticed by many others. Soon I was being asked for advice by business owners and crew foremen within my local area.

It was a moment of clarity.
I realized life as I knew it was about to change for the better . . .

My conditioning had prepared me to recognize an opportunity to serve others. I grew up in the construction business, but my passion has become online marketing, web design, search engine optimization, and social media networking. My new opportunity would be based on my experience and knowledge of business combined with my passion for Internet marketing and social media networking.

I believe that the universe operates full circle
in response to every action being taken.
This is why you must first be willing to give of yourself unconditionally.
Only then will you be asked to receive . . .

All my hard work, constantly conditioning myself, and continuously being proactive in my approach had created such a significant impact that the universe had noticed. Now the universe was actually inviting me to be the social media expert and business consultant I had dreamed of becoming.

I recognized this as an opportunity to share my skills and talents with others by starting a social media consulting business called Shake Hands Online, providing a combination of web design, social media networking, search engine optimization, mobile marketing, and branding services. At Shake Hands Online, our clients obtain a personalized marketing system designed for their needs; all the work required is done for them, while they are able to remain focused on what they specialize in, which is serving their own customers. In addition to all this, Shake Hands Online also offers social media consulting, coaching, and mentoring services to assist clients and their teams in staying up to date with the latest techniques being used to effectively market their business.

I quickly realized that many business owners, their management, and their staff were unfamiliar with the various aspects of these cutting-edge marketing systems. In an effort to better assist them, I immediately began preparing to launch an online membership site called www.ProactiveMarketingSystem.com.

The Proactive Marketing System membership provides world-class training and instructional audio, video, and written materials with up-to-date techniques for producing top results with online and offline marketing campaigns. The Proactive Marketing System membership site provides an opportunity for individuals to educate themselves in how to operate their own marketing campaigns and social media consulting business as well as provide services for others using the same system I use in my own consulting business.

Through the combination of Shake Hands Online and the Proactive Marketing System membership site, I have been able to improve on my ability to serve as many others as possible by providing multiple methods for individuals and businesses to begin implementing the same system I am using to create my own success.

Big things happen when you begin with accomplishing the small details . . .

Baby Steps . . . Walk . . . Run . . .

Establishing myself as an expert within a niche has opened the door to many other opportunities for me to serve others, such as speaking engagements, seminars, webinars, and books like this, where I can share this valuable information with you here today. I thank you for this opportunity. My gift has become my ability to assist, educate, and motivate others to achieve their own goals and dreams. In my heart, true happiness is only achieved when I have the opportunity to assist others with creating their own success in life now that I have found mine.

In conclusion, we must first recognize the importance of conditioning our minds in preparation for the challenges we will face while achieving our future success. This starts by implementing a proactive approach to our education, achieving our personal goals, establishing ourselves within our area of expertise, and serving others. Focus on providing various solutions geared toward assisting potential clients at different price points according to their budgets and needs, therefore maximizing the number of individuals and businesses you are able to serve.

In the end, we must recognize that our own success is achieved not by how well others are able to serve us, but by how well we are able to serve others.

Biography

Edward Brown

EDWARD BROWN has overcome many struggles to become one of those truly inspirational stories, a powerful writer, and a motivational speaker who naturally captures the hearts and attention of those around him and moves them to take a proactive approach to conditioning their own minds and  working toward accomplishing their goals and achieving their dreams. Today Edward finds true happiness in his ability to assist others with achieving their own success now that he has found his own passion in life.

Contact Information

ShakeHandsOnline.org
1-800-ishakehands
ProactiveMarketingSystem.com

Chapter 24

It's Zombie Killing Time

By Harlan J. Wheeler Jr.

I t's a terrible thing to be both the walking dead and the undead at the same time. On one hand, the walking dead don't notice the decay that's happening in their undead life, like loss of passion, loss of direction, and loss of purpose. On the other hand, they also don't notice sunsets, roses, and blue skies. Most doctors agree that once bitten by a zombie, there is no cure. I found out the hard way that there is a cure, but it was no easy task.

Once you become a zombie, the world turns black and white, and you never experience another "first." There is no such thing in a zombie's daily life to ever suggest a "first" will happen again. Zombies are doomed to live a repetitive, boring un-lifestyle.

I think it's safe to say that everyone risks becoming a zombie in today's world. Some people might even have zombie symptoms and not realize that they are under a full-on zombie attack. Zombie symptoms include losing motivation, doing things because other people tell you what to do, and forgetting what your purpose is.

Does this sound like you or someone you know? I was dying a slow death inside each day, but the pain in my heart and soul started out as a dull ache. One day I realized that slowly, without knowing it, I had given up on life. I had forgotten my dreams and just assumed that life was meant to be tolerated. Everyone around me told me this was normal, so I kept trudging on.

It became apparent that my zombie infection started with a series of bad choices. It got to the point where I couldn't run away from these choices, and I guess that is how I got bitten.

I even lied to myself about not being fully infected. I was waking up each day waiting for something to change, only to find my depression was spreading and taking over my life. The sad part is, I made up my mind that I didn't even care because I thought there was nothing I could do about it. I became a full believer in "zombieism."

My friends at the time (who were also part zombie) tried to tell me that things were fine. After all, I owned my own business, I traveled far and wide, and I had a department store worth of zombie toys: a boat, a motorcycle, and some four wheelers. I even had brand new items still in the original store bags, unopened and unused. Zombies own stuff, but they never take the time to enjoy them because zombies have excuses. It's what I call *zombie speak*. These external items made me think that being a zombie was okay.

Then one day I woke up in the hospital. It was about 6 a.m. in January 2006. I woke up in Mount Hood Medical Center to the doctors and nurses asking me about my injuries and health problems. The state police said I had been in an accident. I had come down from the mountain and entered the freeway ramp, and around a corner in the middle of the freeway there had been a stalled car in my direct path with no warning lights on and it was still dark out. My SUV made full contact with the small car, and two people inside immediately lost their lives. Suddenly my zombie mind was torn apart in even more grief than before. It's hard to explain all my emotions. I cried myself to sleep many nights after that. There is even a white wooden cross placed on the freeway at the spot where I hit these people, and I still drive past it all the time.

"God is not supposed to take innocent people over zombies," I would say to myself. At that point in my life, I wasn't even trying to be alive. I was merely existing. Those two people probably had real lives that they loved and enjoyed. I was just getting by on "zombie-time." I'm sure these people had other important people in their lives; everyone who knew me knew I was a zombie. I was not as important as these people.

I left the hospital more emotionally mangled and depressed than ever. During the next year, I was referred to a host of zombie doctors. They all wanted in on the action and gave me plenty of zombie pills to make my mind and my heart pains go away. You'd think there would be a simple warning on those pills: "Don't give to zombies. It will only create a more depressed zombie." But nevertheless, zombies eat whatever you put in front of their mouths, so down they went.

A year after my car wreck, I just couldn't go on un-living as a zombie anymore. Something shifted in me, and I realized I didn't want to take life for granted. I needed a new plan, but how can you stop being what you are? A dog can't stop being a dog. I thought I was doomed! "How does a middle-age zombie get his life back? Nothing good is going to happen to me." That's how zombies think.

I took a step back and realized that the universe's clock is always ticking away at our lives, faster than we could ever imagine. Was this one of God's cruel tricks, setting our stage to live and die in the blink of a cosmic second? Or was this His greatest gift, somehow getting my attention, my epiphany, so to speak? He was speaking directly to me: "You have no right taking this wonderful life I've given you for granted. The clock is ticking!" His reminder was that it's the little things in life that are special, and those little things go a long way. The minute we forget that, we revert back to being a zombie.

I just decided right then and there that I had to change. I woke up to the fact that I had no business taking life for granted, and that morning *I* woke up and changed my attitude to "Do it!" But getting a zombie back to life is no easy feat. I had a lot of work cut out for me. I was 50 pounds overweight, out of shape, with a truckload of bad living habits, from drinking to smoking, and other health problems.

I started out with a healthy food program. I cut out a lot of the processed foods and went to healthy meetings and support groups for people wanting to learn about new power foods (natural and raw foods, organic fruits and vegetables, etc.) Then I hit the gym, slowly at first. I knew not to overdo it. Zombies don't run or do cardio; that's why someone in good shape hardly ever gets bitten. I knew the secrets lay in learning the best workout programs to follow. I started with Bill Phillips' 12-week program, then started with Tony Horton's P90X workout and became a coach for that system.

As my body started healing, I started adding and subtracting what I fed my mind, taking away all that parroting nonsense and disparaging garbage that's rammed down our throats and minds each day and substituting it with only the good stuff, the inspirational and the motivational information. I lived a life of gratitude, and I learned to look at life's magic picture, be it watching the wildflowers dancing in the wind on a beautiful mountain or lying in the grass with the dogs, staring at the silver of the moon.

But I still had trouble believing in myself. Most zombies prefer to die a slow death because they're already dead, and even if you hack away at them with a machete or shoot them, they don't always die. You have to kill their brain or decapitate them. Now this may sound cruel, but after all, that's where all my zombie problems were, in my head. Without a doubt, I knew it was decapitation time.

On my search to figure out the best ways to kill the zombie, I sought out a few coaches who would truly inspire me. One thing I learned is that I couldn't do it alone. These coaches wanted to kill my inner zombie and help me live again. I will tell you this, if you really want to improve yourself and seek success, then get a coach or two. It's their wisdom that I share and pass on with you and others now. Here is what I learned:

1. Coaches will inspire you to believe in yourself, even when you think it's impossible.

2. They will help you define exactly what you want.

3. They will help you create a program to get there or help you know where to look for the resources.

4. They will keep you accountable. This is very important if you want to succeed in anything worthwhile. (As adults we forget this lesson, because there is nobody we're accountable to.)

5. They will help you overcome obstacles that are holding you back.

It wasn't long after working with a few coaches that I finally said goodbye to the pill-pushing zombie doctors who were collecting their big fees. For the next few years, I started combining and teaching the different lessons I had learned from my many different coaches. After seeing me lose lots of weight, my life coach wanted me to share my secrets with him. Then my health coach wanted me to help him with his motivation. They all wanted me to start sharing my story and coaching others. I can guarantee you this, that if you are a zombie person and you want to cure your zombie problems, you need to address the mind, body, and soul as one organism and not three. Most doctors can only treat one area; it's up to you to find the right people to help you address all three.

You've got to set into place small simple steps of proper nourishment for the body, mind, and soul. Even if you're taking baby steps, you'll get there. *"Even a slug on the move can climb a mountain."* Just knowing that you're getting there may be all you need to help overcome your internal zombie battle.

This is what I've done here; I've taken the best from the best and made a program to help zombies reprogram their minds, bodies, and spirits. You will do this by moving little by little in the right direction.

I've now helped many people reach some of their toughest goals. I've helped people stop smoking, lose weight, reach lifelong dreams, and learn how to stay the course from point A to point B. Most important, I've saved them from zombieism and cured them of their zombie life.

My greatest reward in this is seeing the end results, the new person I have helped create, and knowing that I had a small part in the transformation. It took me a few years on this journey to realize that just by giving and sharing my story, I can help so many people. I was destined for greener and greater pastures, and my soul is now on a mission to help others kill their lifeless zombie once and for all.

I feel like one of those actors in the movies—I own a successful business in the daytime, but by night, I'm a zombie killer!

Biography

Harlan J. Wheeler Jr.

HARLAN J. WHEELER JR. is an inspirational thinker, a traveler of imagination, and a successful entrepreneur. A hot-blooded health nut and raw foodist, he is a sharer of experience. He lives on a farm on Mount Hood in Oregon with his wife and his many inspiring animals. His two new books, *Tipping Is a City in China* and *Best Original Inspirational Quotes*, are soon to be released.

Contact Information

3895 Proctor Blvd #362
Sandy, OR 97055
503-622-1726
Harlanmotivates@aol.com
www.zombiecoaching.com

Chapter 25

Ancient Success Secrets of the Rabbis

By Neal Walters

Pirkei Avot, a short collection from "the Rabbis," is known as "The Sayings of the Fathers" or "The Ethics of the Fathers" or even "Chapters of the Fathers." Just as many of the sayings can be interpreted different ways, even the title of this work has multiple interpretations. While *Avot* can be translated "fathers," it can also mean "fundamentals," "principles," or "categories"; thus this short work could also be called "Chapters of Fundamental Principles."

Pirkei Avot is unique in that it is the only tractate of the Mishna dealing solely with ethical and moral principles; there is little or no Jewish law found in Pirkei Avot. The Mishna is dated as a written work around the year 200; however, it was known as oral teachings before that, so many of the concepts date back much further. Most of the other tractates of the Mishna have a corresponding discussion called the Gemara, written in about 500 (most people are more familiar with the collective name of the Mishna and Gemara, which is called the Talmud). However, Pirkei Avot has no such discussion, because its concepts can never be dealt with completely. Nevertheless, numerous medieval and modern commentaries have been written on this amazing collection of sayings.

The tractate effortlessly switches from the heavy and philosophical to the down-to-earth and practical. In this chapter, in keeping with the topic of this book, we will bring to light those principles dealing particularly with personal and business success.

> *1:3 Antigonus of Socho received the Torah from Shimon the Righteous. He used to say: Be not like servants who minister unto their master for the sake of receiving a reward, but be like servants who serve their master not upon the condition of receiving a reward; and let the fear of Heaven be upon you. . . . 1:10 Shemayah said: Love work.*

When you do a job, don't just do it for the money. Do it because you have a passion for the outcome, because you love the work and want to do the best job as a professional. Most people spend eight hours a day, or more, on their "job." If you love what you do, then the time will go fast, and you will be contributing to society. A corollary to this is "Do what you love and the money will follow."

Even though I went to law school at night and passed the bar exam in Oklahoma, computers, software, learning, and teaching were always my first love. Some people do puzzles for entertainment, but I find information technology to be the ultimate puzzle. People pay me to solve their puzzles, and I enjoy solving them.

> *1:4 Yosi ben Yoezer of Tzeredah said: Let your house be a meetinghouse for the sages and sit amid the dust of their feet and drink in their words with thirst.*

Associate with sages, that is, people who are "above" you, whether on a financial, intellectual, or spiritual level. It has often been said that your income will always be the average of the five people you most associate with. The theory is that if your five best friends are millionaires, then you will likely be a millionaire too.

> *1:6 Joshua ben Perachyah said: Provide for yourself a teacher and get yourself a friend; and judge every man towards merit.*

Have you found a mentor or adviser for your project? Why go it alone when others have already been there and can show you the way? Judge others favorably, that is, assume the best in people.

1:7 Nittai the Arbelite said: Keep far from an evil neighbor and do not associate with the wicked; and do not abandon belief in retribution.

This may be obvious, but in business and life, you must be ethical, honest, and above board in all your dealings. People must be able to trust you.

1:9 Shimon ben Shetach said: Examine the witnesses diligently and be cautious in your words lest through them they learn to falsify.

Learn how to read people and avoid the scam artists of the world. Learn body language and Neuro-Linguistic Programming (NLP). Be able to judge someone who is hiring you or selling you the "next best deal." Don't over promise and under deliver.

1:13 Hillel used to say: He who does not increase his knowledge, decreases it. He who learns not, forfeits his life.

Always be learning. Read a book a week, or buy good audio/video courses and learn from them. Many successful people (such as the authors of this book) spend $20,000–$50,000 a year on learning and self-improvement.

Balance your personal success learning with general learning. One of my favorite sources of learning materials is "The Great Courses" (www. TheGreatCourses.com). At least once per year, each course is on sale for 70% off. For most courses, you can select the mp3 downloads and listen on your MP3 player. These courses can make you a more interesting person in conversation. I've taken courses on the U.S. founding fathers, jazz, opera, philosophy, British history, Western civilization, Bible, economics, evolution, and chaos theory. (See my blog at http://NealWalters.com for some of my comments on these courses.)

1:15a Shammai said: Make your study of the Torah a fixed habit.

Wikipedia gives the following explanation of the word *Torah*: "In Hebrew it is derived from the root ירה (yarah) which in the hifil conjugation means 'to teach' (cf. Leviticus 10:11). The meaning of the word is therefore 'teaching,' 'doctrine,' or 'instruction'; the commonly accepted 'law' gives a wrong impression." So in the narrow sense, Torah is the five books of Moses, but in a broader sense it can include many forms of learning.

The point of Shammai's statement here is that it is best to establish a fixed time for study. For example, dedicate 30 minutes each morning. Make an appointment with yourself, and don't break it. If you say to yourself, I'll study after I get the kids to bed *if* I have time, then that means you won't have time. Benjamin Franklin hinted at his weekly practice in his biography: "Sunday being my study day." Imagine if you, like Benjamin Franklin, dedicated one full day of study a week (8–12 hours) on whatever topics interest you.

1:15b Say little and do much, and receive all men with a cheerful face.

Can people rely on you? When you say you are going to do something, do you always do it?

Everybody loves "a cheerful face," and nobody loves a sourpuss. Are you the type of person with whom people want to associate? Be the first to greet someone when you pass them. This is iterated specifically in *4:20. Rabbi Matyah ben Cheresh used to say: Be first in greeting every man. Be a tail among lions rather than a head to foxes.* What does it mean to be a "tail among lions" as compared to a "head to foxes"? Perhaps the modern day equivalent is a "little fish in a big pond versus a big fish in a little pond." You don't want to get eaten by the bigger fish, but you won't learn unless you hang around the big fish (i.e., the lions). Perhaps if Rabbi Cheresh had lived today, he would have been the one that sarcastically said, "If you can't run with the big dogs, stay on the porch."

2:8: The more possessions the more anxiety. . . . But the more Torah the more life, the more schooling the more wisdom; the more counsel the more understanding; the more righteousness the more peace.

Once again, we see schooling and learning being of great importance. It also emphasizes the importance of good counsel. Every successful person will have several people to guide him in various areas of endeavor.

Proverbs 11:14 (King James Version) says almost the same thing: "Where no counsel is, the people fall: but in the multitude of counsellors there is safety."

2:17 Rabbi Yosi said: Let the property of your fellow man be as dear to you as your own.

In business, this verse might be applied to someone who borrows a tool, but especially to one who borrows money.

3:17 Rabbi Akiva said: Tithes are a fence to wealth.

"Tithes" refers to giving money to charity. Why is it called a "fence to wealth"? You build a fence around something you want to keep and protect.

3:21b If there is no flour, there is no Torah; if there is no Torah, there is no flour.

Although the word here is literally "flour," you could substitute the word "livelihood" or "sustenance" (a steady means of support) in this teaching. The concept of Torah potentially means that your work (livelihood) can be a means of purpose and divine service. Your work can be either mundane or inspired, and it's your choice which one you want. Without sustenance, one will have neither the financial means nor the emotional security to pursue intellectual, philosophical, religious, or social endeavors.

4:1 Ben Zoma said: Who is wise? He who learns from all men. . . . Who is mighty? He who subdues his passions. . . . Who is rich? He who rejoices in his portion. . . . Who is honored? He that honors his fellow men.

Meditate for a while on this verse for a variety of applications. But focusing on financial success for a moment, it doesn't matter how much money you make; if you are happy with it, then you are rich. This reminds me of the barber or school teacher who lives within his or her means, saves 10%, and becomes a millionaire, while the person who makes 10 times as much spends it all and has nothing.

4:26-27 Rabbi Yosi bar Judah said: He who learns from the young, what is he like? He is like one who eats unripe grapes and drinks wine fresh from his wine press. But he who learns from the aged, what is he like? He is like one who eats ripe grapes and drinks old wine. Rabbi Meir used to say: Do not look at the flask but at what is in it; there may be a new flask that is full of old wine and an old flask that does not even have new wine in it.

Verse 26 intimates that learning from a young scholar can be biting or sour. The older, more mature teacher has a lifetime of experience and has attained the big picture to back up his teachings. Older people have seen many bust-and-boom cycles come and go and know how to deal with them. Verse 27 reminds most people of the saying, "Don't judge a book by the cover."

This reminds me of the multitude of Internet startups that had big splash grand openings and huge investments but were essentially hype built around no real business purpose. Be sure that your life looks good on both the inside and the outside.

Hopefully you have seen that the Rabbis were wise not only in religion, but also in the ways of life, wealth, and success. Limited space in this chapter means that I had to omit many other success tips of the Rabbis. Visit my blog, http://MrHebrew.com, for additional insights.

Biography

Neal Walters

NEAL WALTERS is an independent software consultant and Microsoft Certified Trainer who has worked in the IT field for 30 years. He develops training courses for both professional software (BizTalk, SharePoint, etc.) and languages (Hebrew and Spanish). With past degrees in accounting, management information systems, and  law, Neal is now pursuing a master of arts in Jewish studies via remote study with Hebrew College. Neal is based in the Dallas area but frequently travels for work.

Contact Information

214-455-8060
NealWalters@NealWalters.com
http://NealWalters.com
http://MrHebrew.com
http://HebrewResources.com

Chapter 26

Success as a Way

By Matt Malouf

What do you think of when you hear the word success? What sort of emotion does it evoke within you? The first reaction most people have when they come across the idea of success is somehow, some way attached to money and finances—that to be successful is somehow having, making, or spending a lot of money. It's no wonder since the bulk of advertising dollars are spent to reinforce this idea of money leading to success when that is often not the case at all. I would even argue that all money really does is bring out who you really are, your true inner person. Having money only brings about the false confidence of being able to say and do things you otherwise wouldn't because of your previous place in society.

We could ask 100 people what it means to be a success and I could guarantee a 100 different answers. A single mom might see success as keeping her children fed and in a good school, whereas a drug dealer might see success as their next big score; a foster child might define success as finding a loving set of adults to adopt him or her into their home. Everyone reading this book right now is at a different place in life, whether it be in work, school, relationships, or just life in general; we all have our own unique skill set and life experiences that contribute to our outlook in life and how we react to both the good and bad life always seems to throw at us. We need to sit down and take a good hard look at ourselves and the TERM (Time-Effort-Resources-Money) we have available and how we can maximize each of those areas to grow and prosper as a person.

Being a success and living a successful life should entail taking care of your whole person, feeding and growing your physical, emotional, and spiritual self. Yes, money is an essential part of life since it helps to keep a roof over your head, food in the fridge, and lights on in the house, but you and your relationships with your family will make that sticks-and-bricks house a home. Success is all about perspective, what your journey in life has been about, whether you've been spoon-fed or struggled a lot. The more struggles you have had, the easier it is to appreciate what you have.

My personal definition of success is to live a full and fulfilling life, the relentless pursuit of a balanced life, where I am comfortable with myself as a person, emotionally, spiritually, and physically. Imagine having all the money you could ever need to satisfy all your desires, then what? What is it that you would do with yourself and your time?

One of the most important things you can do to achieve success is to first surround yourself with people in the proper mindset. Now, I am not suggesting that you try to start hanging out with Donald Trump, but rather that you identify those traits you admire in other people and simply spend more time around those people. Get to know them and what makes them tick so that you can take a little for yourself. Everyone has something to teach you; the point is to open up and listen to them with more than just your ears. Another step is to always, always keep an open mind and be willing to adapt. The only thing we can know for certain is that over time the world changes, so you must at least be willing to adapt and change to it.

The biggest roadblock I have encountered when it comes to limiting personal success is fear. At some point in our lives, we have all experienced what it feels like to be afraid of something; most often it is fear of how others will react to our impending failures and how to cope with that outside influence. The people who truly mean something to you will understand and support you on your journey to success; everyone else is an obstacle that quite frankly should be ignored, which is far easier said than done.

Another step along your journey to success (however you might define that success) is the ability to turn challenges and obstacles into opportunity, to take the experience as a chance to learn something about yourself as well as about the world in which we live. These obstacles that come into our lives every day, some seemingly insignificant and others downright devastating, are our chance to seize the moment and opportunity to grow as people so that one day we can take these experiences and opportunities and turn them into wisdom through reflection.

It is our duty to pass along and share this wisdom with those we love. If you sit down, take a deep breath for a moment, and think about some of the trials and tribulations you have been through in your life—from that first heartbreak, to the feelings of betrayal from a trusted confidante, to losing money on that "sure fire, can't miss" business opportunity, to running that marathon. Something you thought was insurmountable or that you could never accomplish but that you did with hard work, sacrifice, and more often than not a little help and faith from outsiders. You persevered. Life didn't end, and the world kept revolving. You came out with a few bumps and bruises (either emotionally or physically), but you survived, and the universe is telling you something about yourself. Did you listen? Or was that opportunity for growth passed by?

Leadership is another key step in the journey to personal success. As we go through life and experience, all these trials and tribulations, those challenges and difficulties, we must then step into some sort of a leadership role. Now, being a leader does not necessarily mean leading an army of thousands of troops or employees to some sort of Promised Land; rather, it means taking charge of your own actions and first leading the change within yourself that you wish to see in the world. It means to know who you are and what you want to achieve in your life and having the guts to go out and live that life against all odds and obstacles. To lead by example, first define success in your life, then go out and achieve that success and live it out, little by little, day by day. To be a great leader, first be true to yourself and who you are, and then go out and share that person with the world to evoke a change for the better, so that one day you can sit back and feel comfortable and confident that you left the world a better place through your vision and leadership.

The most time-tested quality any leader of any species can possess is courage—not the courage that would lead you to stand up to the playground bully and physically fight your way to victory but the sort of courage to look deep inside yourself and know when it is good to stay and fight and when the time is right to walk away. Often it is a hundred times harder to walk away than it is to stay and fight, win or lose. Courage is looking within you and making the tough decisions based on your core values and beliefs, and then living with the outcome—to stare at those difficult challenges and then somehow turn them into positive opportunities, to eventually sit back and see what the universe has taught you about yourself through these challenges. Many times it is having just enough courage to show up that can make all the difference in the outcome. Mary Anne Radmacher once said, "Courage does not always roar. Sometimes courage is the quiet voice at the end of the day saying, 'I will try again tomorrow.'"

One of my favorite quotes on success is, "If success were easy, then everyone would be doing it." Yet if everyone were successful, then not everyone would deserve it, and nobody would really appreciate it for what the growth teaches you, mostly about yourself. There would then be no incentive to take risks and challenges within one's life to go out and grow and learn.

My role model is George Washington, a man who overcame adversity and turned some of the most difficult times in his life into opportunities, a man who displayed insurmountable courage in the face of challenges, not only from opposing British forces but from potential traitors within his own ranks as well. He stayed true to himself and led with great confidence and compassion.

Remember to always try your best all the time at everything you do, and once in a while, the prize that you get for doing that is coming in first place. Do that and you will always remain a winner.

Biography
Matt Malouf

MATT MALOUF is a Realtor, real estate investor, land-
lord, founding member of the HomeSolutions Realty
Network, certified investment counselor, and specialist in
no-credit and no bank-qualifying transactions. Matt works
as a real estate professional because he has a genuine passion
for real estate and an affinity for people, particularly those
who are in the midst of an important and huge lifetime decision. Being empa-
thetic and listening to home buyers' needs and requirements is crucial to Matt's
ability to marry the right individual with the right property. Matt is a volunteer
at heart and a volunteer in action. It is an honor to be a part of a fellowship
that helps families put their lives back together. Matt pledges loyalty, fairness,
accountability, and determination to all clients and customers.

Contact Information

Matt Malouf Real Estate Investments
10929 Firestone Blvd., #185
Norwalk, CA 90650
909-333-6556
matt@investwithmatt.com
investwithmatt.com

Chapter 27

What Valuable Lesson

By Shelly Barber

My biggest mistake was in believing that what other people told me was right for me *was* actually right for me.

My family fell apart when I was 13, and I decided that I would build my own family to make up for the love that was now missing in my life. And so at 17 I got married and had a baby, despite enormous opposition and pressure. She was a perfect little angel, and looking at her I just knew this was a good plan. When I was 20 I brought my son into the world—another angel. They are two of my greatest teachers.

By 22 I was divorced and on my own, with my two angels. I got a lot of support from my sister and my mum, but it wasn't enough to alleviate the extreme sense of failure that I felt. So I hit the bottle, which stayed my crutch for the next 20 years, until I was finally able to believe in myself fully again and no longer needed it.

I spent those early days running on completely dysfunctional programming—misguided beliefs and values, anger, fear, and guilt. But fortunately, from time to time, I would listen to the little voice inside, and things would tend to work out mostly okay.

That was until the day when the little voice was yelling at me, "DON'T DO IT!" and I didn't listen.

I thought I knew better, and it seemed a great way to make money. I was 27 and still on my own with two children to support, and I *really* needed the money. That became the defining experience of my life. That's the one that led me to my own personal Hell, right here on Earth.

I went into business with my stepdad. Biggest mistake ever! Everything I suggested was wrong. Nothing I did was good enough. I lived with the constant sound of, "You can't do that!" "Don't be stupid," "You can't do that!"

I would go home from work and jump straight into a long, hot shower and scrub my whole body hard to wash the day away. Then I would pour a drink.

I was making reasonable money, though, and I was now in a relationship, so there were now two incomes.

The valuable lesson I learned?—It's *never* worth the money if it's not your heart's desire.

I lasted 12 months, when the catalyst came. I was at home, alone, sweeping my kitchen floor. I had been beset lately by constant bad luck and things going wrong, so as I swept the floor I was swearing and crying and cursing my lot in life.

That was the moment when I remember the words first coming out of my mouth, sobbing, "I want to go home."

Instantly, I heard a voice in my mind say, "So where is home, for you?"

My first thought was, I don't know. The home I grew up in no longer existed, and I had lived in many houses since that time, but I guess for me, home was the last place I could remember being happy.

So I answered, "Bardon. I was happy when we lived in Bardon. Yes, that's the last place I was happy, so that would be home for me."

"And so it shall be."

With that, my decision was made and nothing would stop me. We packed up the family and went back to Bardon, all four of us sitting in the cab of a truck, my partner, my two angels, and me, with all our furniture on the back in a shipping container, very Beverly Hillbillies style.

The business we had was a trucking company, so my stepdad ran the trucks from our depot, an hour's drive away, and I did the accounting from a little room in my home. It was still a daily torture and the bane of my life.

This was when my mum saved me. She bought me out, so I had a little bit of money in the bank, and I trained my replacement.

And just like that, I was *free*. My mum had saved my life. I still couldn't see any light, but it at least felt *possible* now.

So much deep and abiding damage had been done to my fragile self-image, and I had many scars from my time in Hell. They had been very dark days indeed.

As I contemplated those days and my utter failure to achieve success once again, I began to wonder, "Why do some businesses succeed and some fail? What makes the difference?"

This question became a driving force, and I thought that if I understood this, I wouldn't ever have to fail anymore. That thought became my little spark of light in the darkness.

The path of this question led me to a great man, a business builder and coach. He saw some of my work and loved it, so he invited me to work for him. With this great man I learned much about business, and I saw some great businesses fail and some terrible business succeed.

The valuable lesson I learned?—It's not the business that makes or breaks itself; it's the person running it who creates the success or failure.

I loved working with this man and I was learning so much. He was the first person in my world, since I had been a child, who built me up and believed in me, even when I did not believe in myself.

As it turned out, I also had lessons to learn about my personal boundaries. Because I accepted any work he gave me and worked so hard to please, I was burnt out in 10 months of working there and had to leave when my mind gave up and left me completely.

The valuable lesson?—Whether for love or money, never give others more of your time than you are giving yourself. You are the most valuable person in your world, and you must always look after yourself first.

I was now 36, and with the addition of an extra adorable angel, our family had grown to five.

My partner and I had tried multi-level marketing and running our own businesses without success, and now, thanks to my first great coach and mentor, I understood why. It was us! It was something we were either doing or not doing that was keeping success away from us.

There was another gift he gave me—on top of believing in me and supporting me, he encouraged me to be open to things I was interested in to further my learning. So when I found the ad in a magazine for Chris Howard's first ever Breakthrough To Success in Brisbane, I made sure I was there.

That event changed my life in the most significant way yet. Not only did Chris help me to understand how my thoughts and words are creating my world, but I was also given the tools to easily change anything that wasn't serving me and replace my inner programming with loving and empowering values and beliefs about myself, thereby changing my entire experience and the experience of everyone I meet!

Sadly, it also marked the beginning of the end of my relationship, because as much as I wanted us to stay together, I was compelled to follow my path, my purpose, and it was a path my partner didn't want to join me on and a purpose he didn't share.

At that event, Chris helped me to release Anger, a crippling anger that had been my constant companion since my time in Hell, and in a 10-minute process, it was gone! Underneath all that Anger was Sadness, and the tears fell and fell until he helped me to release that as well.

I did every course Chris offered after that, over several years, and there were many more tears as I grew and changed. Now that my Sadness was not being held back only to explode randomly as Anger, I had the opportunity to look at the many events that make up who I am at their root cause, and I now had the tools to let all the pain go forever, with gratitude, love, and forgiveness.

One of the greatest tools I learned from Chris was to write it all out. I learned that getting stuff out of my head and onto paper makes such a huge difference. It clears the thoughts away because I'm no longer storing them and holding on to them. It's such a release and a relief to no longer have the same thoughts going round and round in my head. It's also a wonderful way to have a conversation with yourself to nut things out when you don't want to share the info with someone else or when you have no one else to share it with.

So came my next valuable lesson—Be your own best friend, someone you can trust who understands you and loves you completely. Be your own person you can count on to never let you down.

And so as time went on, I studied successful people in all areas of life: financial, relationships, career, family, health and well-being, business, compassion, and more. I studied what made them who they are, and I took the pieces I liked the best and installed them in myself.

I re-created who I am and who I believe myself to be.

Years and years, studying and learning and re-creating.

Then, 10 years after I had left, my mum asked me to come back to run the business—yes, the same one responsible for my Time in Hell. She had asked me many times over the years, and my answer had always been "NO." I was *never* going back.

But this time she told me she would cry tears of blood if I didn't. Now she was in Hell, and this was a plea for help I couldn't refuse. After all, she had done the same for me—I owed her! I knew what it felt like, and I wouldn't wish it on anyone.

I was a single mum again. My two eldest angels had left home, and now I packed up my little one and our stuff and headed back to Hell to face my demons.

When I walked back in, everything was the same as I had left it, and the most amazing thing I noticed was that *I* was different. It was a *very* different me walking in the door from the one who had walked out all those years ago.

It was made clear from the start that I wasn't welcome, but I was there for a reason—to save my mum from crying tears of blood—and this time I was powerful! I had a personal power and a belief in myself now, and I wasn't going to be pushed around by *anyone!*

So others left instead, and as they left, I employed new people, and I spoke to these new people of hopes and dreams. I knew now that it wasn't the business that caused my Time in Hell—it's just an inanimate object, like money—it was the *people* involved. So I spoke of my plans and dreams and how valuable each person was to me and to this business, and they became my allies, and my friends.

And slowly, against *extreme* opposition from the old regime, together we transformed that business from a grimy, nasty, bullying, back-stabbing, backyard operation into the professional, happy, profitable, and fun world-class business that it is today.

The business has been ranked in the Queensland Top 400 privately owned businesses for the past four years and now provides outstanding passive income for its owners.

My final valuable lesson?—We each have the power to change our world. It just takes one little step . . . then another.

Never let anyone tell you "you can't do it."

Hold your own hand.

Each time you fall, sit back and rest.

Then dust yourself off and get back up again.

Trust that you are here for a grand purpose and never give up.

And remember, things are not always as they seem.

Biography
Shelly Barber

SHELLY BARBER is a serial entrepreneur specializing in transport and business. Shelly has been named an award finalist in both the Professional Business Woman of the Year 2011 and the Professional Manager of the Year 2011 and inspires hope by sharing her story and shining her light to help others find their way to their own personal happiness.

Contact Information

www.trickyfreight.com
shelly@trickyfreight.com
Follow TrickyFreight on Facebook
Twitter: @TrickyFreight

Chapter 28

The Power of Compound Efforts

By Susan Nicely

Are you kidding me? I have the choice of either *a million dollars* or a penny doubled every day for 30 days? That's a no-brainer. You can't really be serious! Who wouldn't take the *million dollars?*

There must be a trick in there somewhere, so I think I will take the penny. Well, after the first week, I have $00.64. I really must have lost my mind to have taken the penny over the million dollars. Okay, okay, it has only been one week. Now after week 2, my total is up to a whopping $81.92. I really am starting to feel sick every time I think of the *million dollars,* and I am about halfway through the month. What did I do?

It is now week 3, and I have jumped up quite a bit—$10,485.76—but that is still a very long way from a million dollars. At least I have something to show for my decision now, and it is not a total loss. But wait! On day 28 an unbelievable thing happens, and my total jumps to $1,342,177.28. Can you believe that I made the right decision? It has been a very stressful 28 days, but I still have a couple of days to go. I think back now to the despair that I felt during those first couple of weeks. There was nothing to show for my choice. And now, are you ready for this? After 30 days the total is . . . are you sure you are really ready? Ta da! The grand total is $5,368,709.12. Truly amazing!

Now, I know what you are thinking: "What does a penny doubled every day have to do with anything except money?" Well, according to Albert Einstein, compound interest is the most powerful thing on earth, more powerful than nuclear energy. That is an overwhelming statement. If you analyze it, you will begin to see what can be accomplished if you continually do a few simple things over and over and over, day after day after day. By putting aside the microwave mentality of needing immediate results, you will discover that unbelievable results can be achieved by simply doing the same simple things every day for a continued period.

Let's take the example of weight loss. We all know that the majority of Americans are overweight. They go on diets to lose those extra pounds, but what happens? They stay on this strict diet for a few days or even a couple of weeks, but they are miserable, and when they don't see dramatic results right away, they quit. Even if they have lost a few pounds, they go right back to their old habits and gain back that weight (and usually a little more).

But what if they were to cut just 150 calories a day from their diet? That certainly is not many and can be done very easily. Of course, cutting 150 calories for a day is not really going to accomplish much, or is it? Do you realize that if you did that for a month, you would cut out 4,500 calories from your diet? Just think if you kept that up for six months—that would be 27,000 calories, which would result in about a 10-pound weight loss. Now, you say, that isn't very earth shattering. No, it's not. But if you were to continue on for a year, then you would lose 20 pounds. Who can't cut 150 calories from their daily intake? A 20-pound weight loss is starting to get significant. If you were in the habit now of cutting out those extra 150 calories, by the end of the next year, you would have lost 40 pounds. Who would not notice that? But did you really miss those 150 calories each day? Did you feel you were depriving yourself? Can you continue on this path? Of course you can, because it is repeating just a simple thing day after day after day!

Just imagine if you use just one hour a day for five days a week to accomplish a simple discipline (for example, making phone calls). Those measly 60 minutes each day equate to 260 hours a year. If you consistently do the same disciplines that are needed for your business for 300 hours, what results do you think you will see? The key to this is to be consistent, every day, every week, every month to equate to compound interest of effort. You have to be willing to do what the average person is not willing to do. Most people are not willing to do these simple efforts day after day after day, and this is why they don't achieve their goals. If you are to achieve your business goals, you must do these same simple things day, after day, after day, and you must be sure that what you are doing is something you love to do so it is not a chore to do it. If you enjoy what you are doing, you will look forward to it, and by doing it over and over and over, you will become a master at it, and your results will double, triple, quadruple, and so forth.

So you basically need to figure out what are the simple things that need to be done every day to achieve your goal. Just pick out two or three disciplines to do each and every day—and they must be done *every day* whether you feel like it or not. That is where you will distinguish yourself from the average person and why you will succeed and emerge a champion.

I am a grandmother who is raising two grandsons, ages five and seven. At my age it is a challenge to have the energy, stamina, patience, and wisdom to deal with these young ones on a daily basis, to provide a financial future for their lives, and to be a great role model. I have found, though, that because I am consistent in providing a loving home with attention and discipline, day after day after day, their lives are becoming happier. The boys are feeling more secure because of the consistent structure in their lives of the same simple things that are done every single day.

Because I have to provide a financial future for these young children, I began studying successful people and their practices. How do you define success? Is it *a million dollars*, or two or three in the bank? Is it having your name be known worldwide? For me, success is having the life I desire. This does not necessarily mean millions in the bank (although that certainly doesn't hurt). I believe success is having the freedom to spend time with my boys, the finances to provide for them and their future, the ability to help others financially and emotionally and still have time to spend with the friends and family whose company I enjoy.

I have found that to have these things, I could not do my activities sporadically, start and stop, a little here and a little there. I never did create much momentum, and when I did and I slacked off, the momentum ceased, and it was so very hard to get it going again. It is definitely hard to not let life get in the way, but the rewards of being consistent day after day after day are unbelievable over time if you just hang in there and don't give up. Remember what your goals and reasons are. Don't forget to review them often, tweak them, and update or change as necessary because they are your motivation. Others you are trying to influence will emulate you, so you must set a good example and be the Energizer Bunny—just keep going and going and going, day after day after day. You will be so amazed after a few months and will praise God that you didn't give up!

How many times have you started something and continued on for a short period, gotten discouraged, and given up? How many times have you seen other people do the same things you were attempting and they succeeded? Did you realize just how close you were to succeeding each time that you gave up? How different would your life be now if you had continued working on that project, job, whatever, and you had achieved the results that you knew were possible? Would you have the freedom that you wanted from your job and your bills? Can you realize now how just a little effort, done consistently daily, can change your life? Have you realized that you need to constantly improve yourself by reading, listening to, and teaching inspirational and motivational materials? Have you realized that what you get by achieving your goals is not as important as what you become by achieving your goals? Have you written down not only your goals but also who you want to become by reaching those goals?

I hope that you will start today doing those few simple things, day after day after day, so that your life will change and you will become the champion you know you can be.

Biography

Susan Nicely

SUSAN NICELY is a very successful entrepreneur, having owned and operated several businesses and completed numerous lucrative real estate transactions. She currently resides in Louisiana with her family, where she is raising her two grandsons, Noah and Jamie.

Contact Information

2005 N. Woodlawn Ave.
Metairie, LA 70001
504-455-7430
nicelydone@cox.net

Chapter 29

Dream Big

By Anne Haritatos

I look at the paradise before me. Luscious gardens, spacious, soaring, light-filled rooms. My beautiful home set in one of the most prestigious suburbs of not only my city, but of America. I pinch myself. Is this real? Is this a dream?

I am again that young farm girl living deep in the African bush, immersed just as deeply in my parents' struggle to farm the land. The good seasons never quite paying off the debts of the bad seasons, and so the steady downward spiral of regret and recrimination. Life was not easy. A new dress or a new pair of shoes was an unheard-of luxury. My five siblings never missed what they had never had—the pretty, useless things, and even some of what many would consider necessities. Their bellies were always full, the one gift of the land, and they loved the freedom of life on the farm. I alone, five years older than my siblings, carried the burden of my parents' hopelessness.

I pinch myself again. No, it is not a dream. Here I am, so many years, so many successes and challenges later, having lived and still living the life of my dreams. I have, with my husband, started over again in two new countries, leaving behind war, injustice, and uncertainty, seeking a better life for our children. We have started, bought, built up, and sold 16 companies along the way. We have raised three great kids with delight and traveled the world with them. I have met amazing people, had the most incredible experiences, and always, I have been thankful for all the blessings received and for the lessons learned.

What lesson did that young girl from the farm learn? To DREAM BIG! Though I did not have much, the one thing I did have were books. Books, the only remaining proof of my parents' affluent life before the farm; books from the boarding school library, books borrowed from friends, books given to me by my uncle, sent from afar on birthdays and every Christmas.

Books are wonderful tools of transformation. They sustained me, opened up new worlds for me, promised me grand new possibilities, fired my imagination, and inspired me to DREAM BIG.

I still today, in my transformational counseling practice, start off my new students with the prompt, "If you could have anything in the world, what would you ask for? . . . DREAM BIG!"

I then say, "Write it down. Write it all down." This is another big lesson I learned. Write down your dreams, your desires, your goals. This brings them into focus, brings them to your attention. You have to think about what you want and be clear about what you want because this is the way you create your life—with intention.

I learned about intention long before it was written about in best sellers and talked about by everyone. It was a very intense two-day seminar on mind dynamics, some 33 years ago in South Africa. The facilitator, Dave Wylie, insisted I write down exactly how I was going to spend the imaginary R100,000 (the South African equivalent of US$100,000) that he had given me. It was a great deal of money at that time. I was new to South Africa, living in a small studio with my husband and our new baby. We had some money, but not much. All our assets that we had built up through seven years of hard work—property, businesses, bank accounts—had to be left behind when we emigrated from Rhodesia. Our assets were frozen by the government, the country still at war.

I nevertheless considered myself fortunate. I had a wonderful, loving, hard-working entrepreneur as my husband and an enchanting new baby, and I knew we would somehow rebuild our life in this new country. "I have everything that is important," I said to Dave Wylie, "I don't need anything." He insisted I spend the money. So I wrote down my intention—to buy my dream home. I clarified all the details and put all my attention on the task. It was to be a contemporary, all glass and concrete, double-story mansion, on the beach in La Lucia—the most prestigious suburb of the city.

That was April 1978, and by June, six weeks later, I was living in that very mansion! The house of my dreams! Through a series of amazing events, a wonderful story for another time, events that I could not have imagined even in my wildest dreams, I was living in the stunning home that I had created in my imagination. It was my home for the next 18 years. There was just one thing that wasn't exact. The house was not on the beach but located higher up on the rising slopes that the suburb was built on, with stunning white water views of the ocean. Years later when I read over my notes from Dave Wylie's course, I saw I had in fact crossed out "on the beach" and written "higher up on the slopes" because I had decided I didn't want all that sand blowing into my home. I still get goose bumps when I recall this.

I learned about the power of intention then. If you are clear about what you want, then all your choices, conscious and unconscious, lead you to your desire. Also, if you know exactly what it is that you want, it is as if the universe bends over backwards to assist you to get it, and miracles happen.

Eight years and many successes later, the greatest spiritual teacher I have known, Stanley Stromfeld, came into my life, and I truly came to understand and appreciate the power of intention. He encouraged me to dream even bigger—not just for myself but for my family, my community, my city, my country, for humanity and for the world. He showed me how to clear my intentions by becoming aware of what I was thinking and examining the beliefs I held, letting go of the limiting ones that were sabotaging my intentions. In so doing, I freed up my attention, the energy that had been used to sustain these untruths from the past, freeing me to be more present. He assisted me to own and deepen my life-affirming beliefs, the ones I chose to live my life by, which naturally supported my intentions.

"Intention plus attention equals manifestation," Stanley used to say. "The clearer your intention and the greater your attention, the easier manifestation."

"And write," he used to urge. "Write it all down. All your thoughts, your desires, your beliefs, your feelings, your realizations, your successes, whatever comes to mind and You will be revealed to you. You will learn the truth of who you are, lumps and all, and be able to let go of what you don't want to be and by the process and in the process, you will clear your intentions, free up your attention, and live the life of your dreams."

I also learned about gratitude from this amazing man—again, long before everyone was talking about it. An important part of his life training, which is what he called his work, was to always write success stories. When any intention manifested, however small or large, I was to write a success story. I had to include everything that I had done to accomplish this success and thank everyone who had contributed to this success, myself included. I always ended up thanking a great many people.

I used to be afraid of flying so I was very diligent in writing clear intentions when taking a trip. I wanted to arrive safely! Safely back on the ground, I found my list of people to thank was long, very long: the pilot, the air crew, the ground crew, the engineers, the air traffic controllers, the caterers, the plane manufacturers, the construction crews (those runways were built by people!), and so on and so on—from the Wright brothers, who made it possible in the first place, to the other passengers whose money paid for it to happen now. We do not live in isolation. Every success we have, we have accomplished with the assistance of many others. Thank them. They will be aware of your gratitude—we are, after all, in the grander scheme of things, all connected—and they will bend over backwards to assist you again. No air traffic controllers fall asleep when I travel!

These wonderful truths I learned so long ago from a great teacher are the truths that I have lived and continue to live my life by. Truths expanded and refined by me, with the contributions of many other amazing teachers, in person and through books. Truths that have brought me much joy, happiness, and success. Truths that have also sustained me through the many challenges that have been part of my journey.

We all crash and burn, tripped up by our own limiting beliefs of what we think life is about or who we think we are, or are not. We create these challenges as much as we do our successes, usually unconsciously. Our hidden limiting beliefs muddy our stated intentions, bind our attention, and then stuff happens, things we do not understand. However, we are the creators of our own reality regardless. This is a powerful wisdom. It means we can undo what we have created if we do not like what we experience, and it only requires that we become more conscious.

So when you do crash and burn, just pick yourself up, dust yourself off, and keep on going in the direction of your dreams. You are the one in charge, and even if at times the journey back to conscious intent and free attention seems onerous, the rewards are priceless—a life of joy, happiness, and success, and the manifestation of all your heart's desires.

That farm girl, from a land far away, is again living in the house of her dreams, in America—the same magic of intention and attention at work, the same truths applied in the manifestation of her heart's desires. On arriving in the USA, the house she, I, had fallen in love with was already in escrow, and it seemed beyond our means. Eight weeks later, through a series of amazing events, another great story for another time, we were living in the house of our dreams!

Play with this magic. It works. Good journeys.

Biography

Anne Haritatos

ANNE HARITATOS was born and educated in South Africa and lived in Rhodesia for many years. She now resides with her husband and family in California. Trained in psychology and several counseling and energy healing modalities, she teaches her students about how life works. She has also, for many years, partnered with her  entrepreneurial husband in their successful business ventures.

Contact Information

858-623-8532
annehari@hotmail.com

Chapter 30

Creating Your Life by Design

By Courtney Carroll

*The degree to which we allow our minds to be consumed by a thought,
whether good or bad, will impact the decisions we make
and the lives we ultimately create.*

What is it that allows someone to rise to seemingly unimaginable heights of financial success while others suffer from lack, poverty, and failure? What keeps some people driving through life toward their destinations (goals they have set), regardless of the obstacles in their way, while others give up at the first sign of trouble? The answers to these questions form the blueprint for the successful construction of a solid financial future.

My early philosophy about money and success was largely influenced by my immediate family and the people in my inner circle. Probably the most influential was my mother, who worked hard to make ends meet but was never confident that she could attract abundance into her life. My mother completed her schooling at the end of grade six and came to Canada to pave a better way for her children.

Our early years were difficult, and my mother worked several jobs to make ends meet. Although we didn't have much, my mom taught us to be appreciative and grateful while in the pursuit of more, a lesson I have never forgotten.

I grew up in the Ontario Housing System (the projects for those of you in the U.S.) and had to make some early decisions about where my life was headed. Negative influences and fast money were on every corner, and you had to have courage to walk away from the trappings of the quick dollar. When I was a child, we were constantly on the move, and by the time I got to grade nine, I had already attended seven different schools. This was a surefire recipe for failure, both academically and socially, but somehow I pushed on and found my way out of that environment despite the bleak beginnings.

In my first year of university, tragedy struck hard. My grandmother passed, my brother was killed in a car accident, and my uncle died four months later from lung cancer—all within the same year. To make matters worse, my mom purchased her first home in 1989 at the peak of the real estate boom. Bankruptcy followed, and the hurt and anger settled in. To compound matters even more, none of my family members had taken the time to prepare for their futures. No life insurance, no investments, and no thought of protecting their families.

I vowed to never let that happen to my family or to the people I loved. I was going to change our family tree, so I got busy working on myself, reading the books, attending the seminars, surrounding myself with successful people, and modeling what they were doing in their lives. I pursued the field of education to inspire, motivate, and empower our youth to believe in their God-given abilities and to walk the road less traveled—to create their lives by design.

So what is success and how do you achieve it?

I have heard many definitions of success, but the one that resonates with me was shared by the late Jim Rohn: "Success is the progressive realization of a worthy goal." The beauty about this definition is that it can be applied to anything we hold as worthwhile in our lives. The key is to be moving toward the goal, not standing still, and certainly not moving in the opposite direction.

For many people, success is defined as having enough financial resources to do what they want, when they want, with whom they want, without apologies. Now, financial success is not the only form of success, but I would challenge everyone reading this book to make it one of the goals you set for yourself because it will not only liberate you from the daily rituals of the masses, it will allow you to bless others in so many ways.

So how do we get there? How do we achieve the level of success that is our natural birthright? We must understand and adopt some key steps to achieve any noteworthy level of success in our lives.

Those who are truly successful *have a crystal clear understanding of what they want to achieve in their lives.* They can see it, smell it, touch it, and hear it because they have taken the time to write it down and hold it at the front of their conscious minds until it materializes in their reality.

Napoleon Hill's *Think and Grow Rich* speaks volumes on the importance of having a clearly defined goal. He goes on to define it as having a burning desire and definiteness of purpose about what you want to achieve in your life.

So having a clearly defined goal or an intention for what you want to do is the first step. So what is your intention? What vision do you have for your future? When people read your obituary and congregate at your funeral, what will the dash between the date you were born and the date you die say about your life and the contributions you made? What legacies will you leave behind? Or will you go quietly like the millions who leave nothing but liabilities for their families?

Once you have set and written down a clear goal for yourself, you need to take the second step in the process: *Make the commitment to never give up until you achieve your goals.* Successful people keep their word, and once they commit to a goal, they do all that is necessary to achieve it.

If you have a clearly defined goal but have not committed to going after it, you will never achieve success. The trouble with most people who fail is that they see obstacles as road blocks, while successful people see obstacles as an opportunity to grow and find new solutions to a temporary setback.

Obstacles are not meant to stop you from achieving your goals; they are a test to see how badly you want to achieve your goals. Break through those obstacles and stay committed and the universe will yield to your desires.

Years ago I set the intention to create financial freedom through real estate, and I committed to seeing it through. No one was coming to my rescue with an inheritance or a winning lottery ticket. If it was going to happen, it was up to me. I was 100% percent committed to this goal because I believe strongly in the integrity of my word. Successful people will commit to something only if they know with certainty that they wish to. I was committed to this goal because it would allow me to create the life I had always envisioned for myself. It would allow me to bless others and leave legacies behind when I die, not only for my family but for my communities.

The third step in the process is to *have a clear plan* for how you will achieve the success you are seeking. Successful people have the foresight to develop a contingency plan in case things don't work out. You are committed to the goals you have because there is value in what you are trying to create. You are committed because you know your success will uplift your family and community and force you to tap into your creative genius and God-given potential, but without a solid plan for how you will achieve it, you will fail.

If your goal is to have real estate as your investment vehicle, what does your plan look like? What will be your specific strategy? Are you going to purchase for cash flow, appreciation, and equity or fix and flips? Who will be on your team and how will you go about finding them? Are you planning to purchase these properties as an individual investor, a corporation, or with business partners?

Your plan irons out all the details so you can work on your business successfully. Without a clearly articulated plan for success, you are just shooting in the dark, hoping to hit your target.

Your plan provides a clear focus for whether you are on track. The beauty about your plan is that it can be tweaked here and there as new challenges come your way. It provides peace of mind and will get you to your goals much quicker, provided it is a good plan to begin with.

So now you have clearly identified the goals you want to achieve, you have made the commitment to go after them, and you have a workable plan that allows for flexibility as needed. *The next step for success is to take action.* The best-laid intentions without action are merely dreams. Are you willing to take the actions necessary to elevate your life and play at the next level?

It is great to go to the seminars and read the books, but all the theory in the world won't get you to the next level until you are willing to act. Through actions and the willingness to get uncomfortable in your own skin, the miracle of success begins to take shape.

I have sat in many seminars with people who tell me they are real estate investors. On closer observation, I find that they are seminar junkies who attend one seminar after another without ever taking action. They are learning from some of the best mentors in the real estate business, mentors who have achieved financial freedom and are living the lives they hope to live. Yet despite the wonderful teaching and modeling available, these individuals never get off "ready, set." Successful people understand that you cannot change your life if you do not get out of the starting blocks. If you are willing to take the first step and trust, the way will be revealed to you.

When I purchased my first investment property, I didn't have a clue what I was doing. I quickly realized that it was not my business to know exactly how it would be done. My only concern was how to take the first step. I didn't need to know all the steps in the process. Once the first step was taken, I quickly learned what was required for the second step, then the third, and so on.

In addition to having the courage to act, I was very fortunate to have the guidance and support of good mentors around me. Paola Breda of Canadian Financial Freedom helped me work on my mindset and confront and overcome the limiting beliefs of my early philosophy about wealth and success. Once I broke through those limiting beliefs, my world opened up, and I started making deal after deal, each one teaching me something new about the world of real estate investing.

The fear of the unknown paralyzes many people from taking the action needed to improve their lives. They would rather stay comfortable and content with what life gives them than take from life what they truly deserve. Don't follow the masses. The quickest way to conquer fear is to take action. Are you willing to pay the price up front and in full so that you can live a blessed life? Part of that price is having the courage to act despite fear.

The final step for achieving success is to *stay the course.* Do not get sidetracked or give up on your dreams. Understand that this is a long-term commitment. You have to be willing to repeat the process until you form the habits necessary for success.

We live in a microwave society, where many people want results immediately. They forget that there is a cultivation period between the planting of the seeds and the reaping of the harvest. People who fail often forget to nurture the seeds they plant. They are looking for the overnight success. Unfortunately, there is no such thing as overnight success. Success takes 10 to 15 years before it will materialize in your reality, and that is if you nurture the seeds you've planted.

Those who fail in life are quick to give up after the first signs of failure. They are not willing to adjust their sales, tweak their plans, and keep trying. Successful people understand that the probability of success increases exponentially each time they meet with failure and are able to bounce back. They surround themselves with people who share their vision and have an unwavering commitment to their dreams.

So are you ready to play at the next level? Are you willing to join the top 5% and live the life of your dreams? Changing your life is certainly not easy, but easy is not an option. Successful people are willing to do what is hard so that their lives will be easy, while those who do what is easy will find their lives to be extremely hard.

As you absorb the teachings in this book, I challenge you to commit to paying up front the price for success so that your life will be easy. You were put here to make a significant contribution with your life and to leave legacies behind. You are equipped with all the tools needed to co-create an incredible life and to bless others. Set your dreams in the sky, commit to their achievement, put a solid plan in place, work your plan, take decisive action, and stay the course. If you are willing to follow the steps outlined here, you will achieve the goals you have set for yourself regardless of how lofty they might appear to others.

Biography

Courtney Carroll

COURTNEY CARROLL is a principal with the Toronto District School Board. He is a successful real estate investor, an author, and a professional speaker. Courtney believes we were put here to serve others and is passionate about teaching the success principles that have allowed him to elevate his life and create a financially fit future.  Courtney is available to serve you and your organization as a speaker, trainer, or success coach.

Contact Information

1228 Huntingwood Drive
Toronto, Ontario, Canada M1S 1K8
www.thefinancialfitnesstrainer.com
www.courtneycarroll.com
Courtney@thefinancialfitnesstrainer.com
647-967-9876

Chapter 31

Walk in Success

By Torrence Roundtree

Success is defined as an outcome, a result, a degree or measure of succeeding, a desired outcome, the attainment of wealth, favor, or eminence, one who succeeds. Personally, I like Zig Ziglar's definition of success: "having the ability to measure not by the material things you possess, but . . . by what you have accomplished to what you *could have* accomplished." I didn't know what success was growing up. Sure, I played sports, and I was on championship teams. I never thought about those wins as successes. I didn't celebrate those championships as if they were my own; I just didn't see it that way. Oh yes, I was happy during those times; I just didn't know how to really celebrate *my* successes as a child or a young adult. I simply saw them as good times in my life.

Now that I am older, I realize that I did not have a mentor or a role model to follow. I didn't know I needed someone in my life to show me how to create success. Truthfully, at that time in my life, I did not consider success as an option for myself. I was brought up to think in terms of the 40/40 plan: 40 hours per week for 40 years working for someone else. The 40/40 plan was a way of being in my family; it was all we knew. I didn't know I needed to build relationships, network, and surround myself with successful people. I just didn't *know*. Oh, I had both parents in the home, but they were young and still trying to find themselves, so they had no solutions to offer. Had I known how to reach out and seek the right guidance, maybe some of my frustrations could have been avoided. Looking back, my past was predicated on basic survival skills; possibilities were not in the realm of my comprehension.

I was around 12 years old when I decided I needed to make changes in my life. This is when I began to feel that I wanted more out of life than I was accustomed to. I wanted to become something different than what I saw in my environment. Many of the people who lived there never made it out. Those who did appeared to have something the rest of did not have—direction and support. In many cases, we have to leave our current environment in order to grow and expand. Limiting environments or people with limited beliefs will cause you to live at a much lower standard than what you're truly capable of. The one thing I knew for sure is I didn't want to live any less than what I was capable of. I wanted to accomplish all that I could.

So as I look back on my life and the successes that I never celebrated, I wonder what happened to lead me to where I am. I grew up on the south side of Chicago. Needless to say, my environment had its challenges, from lack of financial resources to poor schools and broken families. For me this was a normal life; it was my view of the world. What I could not reconcile in my mind was the disparity that I saw among the families in my neighborhood. I saw that some families lived better than others. Did those parents aspire to live differently? What made them seem so successful? What was their incentive that drove them to be more successful than the next? What did they have that my parents did not have? Was it more education, more desire, more self-confidence, more resources, what?

As I entered high school, my perspective on life began to change. I began to see more opportunity for myself, although nothing changed in the way I thought about success because I had no foundational success principles to build on. For the first time, in my junior year, I began to shape my future, thanks to my high school counselors. I began to make decisions that would ultimately change my life. I no longer wanted to be a police officer, fireman, or postal worker. By this time I knew I could be, do, and have more. When asked the question, What did I want to be in life, I proudly responded, electrical engineer or mathematician.

As I began to identify with what I wanted to become and the possibility of that desire coming true, I began to believe in my goals and my future. I began to share my optimism with people I felt close to. I noticed a change in people as I shared my vision; they wanted to spend more time with me. They wanted to hear what I had to say. People began to help and reach out to me. Things were changing in my life, but I was unaware of how significant these new possibilities were. I was just living!

I had a friend whose mom helped me get my first summer job. Her company was hiring senior high school kids to work during the summer. She would take me to work with her in the mornings and bring me home when the shift ended. What was most interesting to me is she did not refer her own son for employment, but she referred me. She saw something in me that I did not see in myself: Success! She saw that I had hopes and dreams. If she could see this in me, why couldn't I see this in myself?

It wasn't until I was 18 years of age that I really began to face life's challenges. One of my biggest decisions was to go to college. This was when I took full control of my life. I experienced more successes at that time than at any other time thus far. I started making decisions and choices that I had to stand by. Here again, I did not have foundational principles to help me see how things affected every area of my life. For instance, I received athletic scholarships and most improved football player of the year, was scouted, and participated in the first ever NFL combine, yet I had no idea of the value of these accomplishments and how I could have used them to leverage myself for more. What a missed opportunity! Instead, I chose to leave college prematurely and get married.

During this transition of leaving college and caring for a family, I began working for a major corporation. A manager took interest in me and spoke to me about my future. I said to myself, someone is beginning to take notice of me. This was a feeling I had never experienced before, and I liked it. We talked about my value and the contribution that I was making to the team. We discussed ways to improve my skill set to increase my value to the team; but most important, this was my first introduction to mentorship. He explained what a mentor was and the role a mentor plays in your professional career. Remember, I didn't think I needed a mentor. I didn't know what a mentor was at this time. Now I know! Wow, I was in the dark for a significant portion of my life.

Well, let me tell you, he trained me on how to maintain a level of *desire* and positive thinking. Even after his teachings, I was still lacking in this area because I didn't understand the value of what I was being taught. All I knew was it was different than anything I'd ever done before.

My mentor wanted to know what I was most passionate about. Guess what? I didn't know what I was passionate about anymore! I had wanted to be an electrical engineer, but I'd left college early, so I was back on the 40/40 plan without even knowing it. Once again, I was faced with the reality of no foundation, no direction, going through life aimlessly without purpose. This reality caused me to make irrational and costly decisions in my life. But I learned that maintaining focus is a critical factor for success, because being focused allows you to move through life with a deliberate intent on accomplishing your objective. Lack of focus creates the relentless spin cycle of high effort with zero results.

As a result of being mentored for several years in Corporate America, I learned how to apply critical success characteristics to my life.

- Reflect daily.
- Gain insight from your experiences.
- Celebrate successes (big and small).
- Remain focused on and committed to your objective.
- Seek guidance—get help when needed.
- Be persistent—this is key.

Again, I had to regain control of my life and the decisions that I made. As I began to reflect on my past, I went back and celebrated past successes (such as my sports championships, my scholastic degrees, my first start-up business, my family, and my marriage). These were a few of the eventful and successful times in my life. The steps I take now to maintain my successes are as follows: I remain *competent* in my industry, and I stay *committed* to my tasks. I find *coaches* who are successful in my space, and I do what they do; I leverage the knowledge base of those individuals. I have learned that self-development is essential to my future success.

Even to this day I remain focused, and I don't allow anything to stand in my way. Many times we allow negative feelings and thoughts to rule our lives, and we allow negative people to rule us as well (this could be a spouse, a good friend, a job, a physical ailment, a family member, or yourself). When we stay true to our beliefs and fight our best fight for our dreams, the universe will yield to our aspirations and our ambitions.

Why it is so important to be persistent with your desire and thoughts?

We live in a world where we are *all* connected. We give power to the things we think about the most; whether those thoughts are negative or positive, we give life to them the more we think about them. It's the law of the universe, like attracts like: successful people attract other successful people; leaders attract leaders. I now surround myself with positive, strong, and clear-thinking people.

I am so much more aware of what it takes to be successful. You can't do anything in isolation, which is the mistake I made for so many years—you need people to help guide you along the way. Be open and seek help: *Where there is no counsel, the people fall, but in the multitude of counselors, there is safety* (Proverbs 11:14).

In conclusion, always work on you, invest in yourself, and find someone who can coach or mentor you to help you achieve your desires. Remember that what you think about, you bring about. To be successful you have to work at becoming successful; you must think and believe that you are successful even if you're not. Stay focused and committed to your dreams. When you lose focus and change direction, you produce recurring negative results. Measure how successful you are by reflecting daily on yesterday's tasks or activities.

Beginning right now, walk in success as if you are the most successful human being on this earth. When you start controlling your thoughts and desires, you begin to attract those things that you focus on the most. You control what is manifested into your life. The power of intention is what you use to bring about your desires. So feel good about being successful, feel good about working hard, and be aware of your thoughts. When you're giving thought to your desires, always remember to ask for what you want, believe that you will get it, and receive it as if you already have it. Never allow your ego to be the stumbling block of your success: *Get out of your own way!*

Biography

Torrence Roundtree

TORRENCE ROUNDTREE has 26 years of experience in Corporate America. His skill sets expand across multiple disciplines in the world of business, from sales and marketing to information technology. The past 10 years, Torrence was employed as an IT Project Manager II, implementing ERP solutions throughout the John Deere Corporation.

Since leaving John Deere, Torrence has gone on to become an entrepreneur, establishing his own IT company, Fortrees Business Solution. In May 2011, Fortrees Business Solution was asked to join the Global Branch Initiative Team, which was created to implement standard processes across the company's global platform. Torrence will help enable processes across Brazil, Russia, China, India, South Africa, Australia, Mexico, and Poland. He is now in a position to help people understand the meaning of being successful. If you care to further your growth and learn more about the content in this chapter, he is available for one-on-one business and life coaching sessions.

Contact Information

2731 NC Hwy. 55, Ste. 246
Cary, NC 27519
888-613-7455
Torrence@torrenceroundtree.com
www.sustainingsuccess.com

Chapter 32

Look Inside
Your Soul for Success

By Philip Rees

My parents met when they started kindergarten at age three and progressed through school until Bishop Gore Grammar school and Greggs Technical College separated them. In their late teens they met again, married, and started their working lives together. My father had to move to different locations to progress in his career while my mother was a highly skilled personal assistant.

This background not only led to exciting times, moving schools and finding new friends but also presented difficulties, as I was easily identified as the boy born in Ferndale, Rhondda, South Wales, who talked differently from my classmates. This served to develop my communication skills early in life so that I avoided a lot of bullying. Sometimes shyness is a defensive strategy for survival.

My secondary school was my fifth school. I worked diligently for the first two years to reach the local grammar school but was narrowly defeated in my aim by a friend whose casual attitude to his success meant that he did not capitalize on his place and fared no better than me. My schooling came to a halt when my father accepted promotion, which meant another move. Unfortunately, it meant that it was not possible for me to progress to the second year of advanced levels because the subjects were not available to me. As I wanted to follow in my father's footsteps, I started working for Barclays Bank at our new location.

After nearly six years working at various branches, meeting hundreds of colleagues and customers, I was at a crossroads in my working life. The direction that banks seemed to be taking in the late 1970s was too driven by selling and not servicing the needs of customers, I thought. I was tired of snide remarks that as a bank manager's son, I was going to be all right. I wanted to stand on my own two feet.

That viewpoint coupled with changing my car led me to an opportunity to help the car sales entrepreneur administer his business. Six months after I left the bank, a downturn in trading meant I found myself redundant—in that week we learned that we were expecting our son, Jonathan. I found suitable employment at the personnel section of the Royal Mint in Llantrisant.

A car dealership approached me with a position administering sales so I left the Royal Mint to work at Tonyrefail Motors Limited, a successful family-owned company that tried to maintain headway despite downward trends in sales in that industry. As expansion receded, I found myself in the group accountant role, restructuring costs to ride out the turbulent economy of the mid '80s. Preparing the accounting justifications for laying off a third of staff was a heavy task for me and one that saw me leaving for a new venture. This time I took a programming course in COBOL. Although I completed the course, I had no degree at that time, and employers wanted only graduates. I resolved to correct my lack of a degree, but the B.Sc. infomatics degree I wanted to take was not approved, so I had to wait nine months before my business studies teachers' course commenced.

As I was very aware of the support I had to train as a teacher of business studies and as I had been unemployed for nine months since the programming course, during my four years of study, I volunteered to assist with the Samaritans, an organization that provides a listening ear to those who seek help at times of despair. Helping others less fortunate than oneself is a reminder of how much support one has from friends and family. I was blessed and wanted to share with others in difficult times. To this day, though, when I get a bill, I still wonder if I have enough in the bank to pay it, as the scars of being unemployed remain deep.

For the final year of my B. Ed. (Hons) business studies course in Swansea, I moved my family to Swansea so that our son, Jonathan, and daughter,

Emma, could benefit from their formative education in my adopted home. Swansea was where my parents were born and also my wife, Judy. Indeed, our children attended the school my wife had in Danygraig and were able to start their secondary education at Bishop Gore as my father had.

On graduation, I could not find a teaching post, so I returned to commerce, eventually working for Kenji Suyama at Orion Electronics in Port Talbot. I admired his dedication and his work ethic. At the request of a good friend, I left so that I could help administer his business. After a while, I had my first teaching post at Hawthorn High School in Pontypridd, north of Cardiff, situated as a gateway to the Rhondda valleys, where I was born. The headmaster, Kevin Mullins, was inspiring as he would advocate that we all look outside ourselves to realize we are all part of something bigger than just ourselves. I owe most gratitude, though, to Dave Matthews for guiding my career.

I have learned that to succeed in life, you have to dare to be different and be human enough to care about those you meet on your journey. Look inside your soul, hear your own heartbeat, and find there who you are and who you want to be. Work at what you like about yourself and put negativity behind you. For me, the measurement of success is to arrive at our destination without harming others along the way, assisting others instead, as many will assist us in our journey. The key for me lies in accepting change, looking forward with focus and drive, leaving negativity in the past, and having faith.

Whatever setbacks I have encountered in my life, they have helped me to be the person I am today, so I have learned to accept them for the valuable lessons and insights they have given me and hopefully learn from them to improve myself as a person. When my students had a particularly difficult time, I would remind them that in life we can throw boomerangs, and if we don't catch them as they come back to us, they can decapitate us. Life is not a cycle but a spiral. When we learn one lesson (which may come back at us until we do learn from it, like a boomerang), then we progress to the next level and learn from that one and so on, moving forward to our destination.

When I reach my destination, I hope that I can look back and see that I have learned enough to pay forward the help and assistance I have had so that others will have had my help when they need it. In so doing, I hope to pay my way in this life doing to my fellow creatures as I would hope they would do to me. When I taught IT/ICT, lessons about life most helped some of my students at their times of difficulty. To see someone coming to terms with their place in life, for them to see their way forward, is a reward beyond measure for an educator. Often it helps to see not the daunting tasks ahead but looking back from the destination at accomplishments along the way to envision how challenges may be overcome.

As a teacher I was privileged to meet many students. One in particular inspired me in the manner of his facing his difficulties. I was a form tutor at Sydney Russell School, Dagenham, under the inspiring headship of Roger Leighton when I was privileged to meet Luke Fullerton, who had multiple sclerosis and knew that his life expectancy was not to see adulthood. At age nine, he lost his best friend and determined with the help of his parents to establish his own funeral service, and what a joyous celebration he prepared for us. He taught me a great deal about facing up to life and making the most of it.

Luke Fullerton 9UD

Last Thursday night Luke left us. His fight over, dignified in death as in life, he won the right to rest in peace.

He left us with fond, happy memories to treasure for the rest of our days. In our memories he lives on—our hearts touched by his happy smiling face and boyish grin, his humanity, his sense of humor and his love of life.

Luke suffered problems with his health, but he never let them get in the way of living his life to the fullest he could. He was one of life's fighters and showed us all how to live our lives in dignity, to the full.

In life, Luke was respected; in death, regretted. I will not mourn but rather celebrate and treasure his precious memories for the rest of my days, hoping I can live up to his rare example of not being sad about the difficult things that life throws our way, but being glad to be alive and to live life to the full. I would like to think Luke would have wanted that for all of us.

Mr. P Rees (Form tutor) 10/07/2004

For inspiration about leadership, I am reminded of the lines from the poem "If" by Rudyard Kipling:

> If you can keep your head when all about you
> Are losing theirs and blaming it on you;
> If you can trust yourself when all men doubt you,
> But make allowance for their doubting too.

A leader, in my mind, should have vision and determination to achieve that vision while guiding others in achieving theirs. Some lead from the front, others from behind, and some move along the line checking that others are not under undue strain. A leader should not be afraid to show his or her humanity and care for others along the journey so that everyone arrives at the desired destination. The qualities a leader should have are determination and focus to see the task finished but the humanity to achieve journey's end by helping others along the way as well as the faith in oneself to see the way forward, even though others may not. Lead without fear of failure. Indeed, see failure or success as illusions because the manner in which we arrive at our destination is important.

My favorite quote is to misquote Arthur C. Clarke: I NOT robot. Why? Because I am human just like everyone else ever born and still to be born. I am free to make my own way in this life, and I will. Hopefully, I will remember my humanity and that of my fellow creatures as I journey through life seeking my success, not at the cost of others but by my own merit, as I am free to do.

My father, Elvan, has been my inspiration because in parallel with his career in the bank, he also squared the circle and served society as a lay preacher strongly supported by my mother, Valerie. I am mindful of the verse by Dorothy L Sayers often quoted in child care settings: "If a child lives with encouragement he/she learns to find love in the world."

At this moment in my life, I have retired due to ill health with COPD, but I have fond memories of my time at Oaks Park High School, Ilford, under the superb headship of Steve Wilks. It leaves me, aged 57, to seek out ways of making a living to pay off a mortgage and other loans, though sometimes I am confined at home through bouts of breathing difficulties.

As I seek out a new path, my inspiration is Joel Therien, who founded many successful businesses, and by grace of providence I saw his opportunities and training. It has been life changing as he has introduced me to people such as Mike Glaspie, Joel Peterson, Matt Morris, Chris Reid, Mike Potvin, and Mark Call. Finally, you, dear reader, inspired me to write my story to share with you. I hope you also have inspiration in your life and seek your success too. Travel well.

Biography
Philip Rees

PHILIP REES is a father of two, a commercial administrator, and an educator with interest in computing technologies. He is currently developing online and offline businesses with an interest in webinars and Internet marketing.

Contact Information

+447811833064
p.rees@reesservices.co.uk
http://philiperees.com

To receive over $2,000 in free bonus gifts
for purchasing this book, visit

www.SuccessYouPublishing.com/gifts

CPSIA information can be obtained at www.ICGtesting.com
Printed in the USA
BVOW021751310112

281834BV00005B/5/P